THE WELFARE MOTHERS MOVEMENT

A Decade of Change for Poor Women?

Susan Handley Hertz

UNIVERSITY
PRESS OF
AMERICA

For Tom, Karen,
and Christopher

iii

TABLE OF CONTENTS

CHAPTER

CHAPTER 1

Introduction

The proliferation of social, political, and religious movements is a dramatic feature of the recent history of the United States. These movements are distinctive because of the identity of those whose interests are being expressed and because of the methods they have used. Despite our image of American society as a "melting pot," many ethnic, racial, socioeconomic, and other groups are now demanding that their differences be recognized and that they be allowed to participate in the political arena on their own terms.

One of the groups which emerged between 1965 and 1975 came from the previously unorganized segment of our population made up of women receiving Aid to Families with Dependent Children (AFDC). By 1970, a set of loosely interlocking local and national organizations of welfare mothers had emerged across the country constituting what can be called the Welfare Mothers Movement. The organizations within this movement tried to develop new options for welfare mothers, change the public stereotype of the welfare recipient, or develop a new sense of group identity in order to bring about changes in the local and national welfare systems. To achieve these goals, welfare recipient groups employed tactics ranging from encouraging self-help activities to lobbying legislators and engaging in militant demonstrations. The opportunities and constraints encountered by welfare mothers in the United States as they tried to unite politically and attain their goals is the subject of this book; its specific focus is on the development of the Welfare Mothers Movement in the state of Minnesota.

Three major themes will be developed in analyzing the Welfare Mothers Movement: (1) the effect of the double handicap of their sex and poverty on the political activities of welfare mothers; and (2) the consequences of their involvement in a

social movement--to most Americans an unfamiliar
and somewhat perplexing form of social organization; and (3) the impact of the historical, institutional, and contemporary political contexts on
the expansion and contraction of the Welfare
Mothers Movement.

Poor Women

First, welfare is a woman's issue as well as a
crucial economic issue for the women of all races
and their children who depend on AFDC for their
livelihood (Tillman, 1972 quoted in Johnson &
Holton, 1976:175). Much of the anthropological
literature on culture and sex roles indicates that
American society makes a "clear sex-marked distinction between the 'outside,' male world of work,
politics and war, and the 'inside,' female sphere
(Garretson, 1976a:197). Likewise, Rosaldo
(1974:23-4) contends that:

> An opposition between "domestic" and "public"
> . . . supports a very general identification
> of women with domestic life and of men with
> public life. These identifications, them-
> selves neither necessary nor desirable,
> can all be tied to the role of women in
> child rearing; by examining the multiple
> ramifications [of women's place in the psych-
> ological, cultural, social, and economic
> aspects of human life], one can begin to
> understand the nature of female subordina-
> tion and the ways it may be overcome.

Cross-cultural evidence suggests that women are at
a particular disadvantage in competing for power
and prestige precisely in those societies (such as
our own) where a large separation between the
domestic and public spheres is found. In the political systems of such societies, where decisions
are reached outside the home and where leadership
rests on the control of resources largely available
only to men, women are often found to be excluded
from direct political participation. Confined
to the home (ideally, if not actually) and often

2

defined as legal minors or childish and incapable, women must work in concealed ways to attain their ends and their efforts to achieve public power are discouraged and regarded as disruptive (Collier, 1974:91-2).

The political disabilities experienced by all women in our society are amplified by poverty. Particularly on the local level, public political activities by welfare recipients (whether male or female) have traditionally been discouraged. Informal political custom has relegated political representation of welfare mothers to the welfare system in what may be characterized as a patron-client relationship.[1] It has been welfare officials and the professional social work community, not recipients, who have designed and proposed welfare statutes and grant levels and who have represented their clients in state legislatures and the Congress (Hertz, 1978:124). In many ways the poor are subject as well to a different legal system than are the affluent in the United States-- often being denied the "constitutional guarantees of the equal protection of the laws, due process of the law. . . the right to privacy, and the right to counsel [e.g., in termination hearings] (tenBroek, 1970:357).

The traditional female roles of economic and social dependence referred to by Garretson and Rosaldo are also reinforced by a woman's involvement with the welfare system. In particular, the welfare system controls the participation of poor women in the labor market by making AFDC eligibility contingent on the recipient's acceptance of employment, usually without regard to minimum wage, by restricting welfare mothers' access to higher education and job training programs, and by limiting the availability of day care services. "Thus the welfare system does in fact control all those factors vital to the employment, survival, and autonomy of poor women" (Johnson & Holton, 1976:173).

Economically, the welfare system is not only the source of the recipient's livelihood, but also mediates her relations with the commodity and credit markets of the larger economic system. For example, the poor have more difficulty getting loans or credit, and public transactions involving vendor vouchers, food stamps, and the distribution of commodities differentiate her from others in the marketplace. Often a recipient's relations with landlords and employers are monitored by her welfare worker (Jacobs, 1970).

Sacks (1974:221) and Sanday (1974:200) have both persuasively argued that economic factors are the main barrier separating women from greater participation in the political system. In general, working in the public labor force ("real" work with exchange value, i.e., for wages), producing for public consumption, or owning property are necessary but not sufficient conditions for the development of political power. Middle- and upper-class women may fulfill one or two of these conditions; welfare mothers fulfill none.

Furthermore, political and economic constraints are buttressed by public (and often academic) stereotypes which serve to separate the dependent poor from the rest of our society on the basis of supposed subcultural differences in values and behavior (cf. Valentine, 1968). For example, the poor are stigmatized as inadequately socialized in the American values concerning work, family life, sexual behavior, and education. In addition, the decision to accept public assistance may mean that a woman is ostracized by neighbors, friends, and even her family. This social isolation may be reinforced by physical segregation, since many welfare mothers move from their original homes to public housing projects, ghettos, or "Model Cities" areas where low-income housing is available (Hertz, 1978:125). As Beck (1970:67-8) points out:

> There is a certain formal similarity between our relationship to the poor and the relationship of expanding European societies to the "aboriginal" populations which turned up as embarrassing by-products of the inclusion of new territories in their spheres of activity. In spite of the most admirable

4

attitudes we can muster, the poor remain "our
natives," in the strongest senses of each of
those words. . . . To be poor is no longer
to be one of us. Intervention in their
affairs becomes noble, instead of rude.

Social Movements

In much of the social science literature of the
1950s and the 1960s, radical political, social or
religious movements were seen as results of or
reactions to social disruption and personal dis-
orientation. One corollary of this perspective
was a negative evaluation of movement participants.
For example, groups attracted to social movements
were assumed to be suffering from social disorganization, deprivation, or psychological maladjust-
ment. Alternatively, Eric Hoffer (1968) suggested
a "fun and games" theory of movements to explain
the involvement of affluent, well-educated, and
clearly capable students in the Student Movement
of the early 1960s (Gerlach & Hine, 1970:xii-iv).

For many Americans, the "disorganization" of movement participants is reflected in the perception
of social movements themselves as collections of
unrelated, disorganized and seemingly leaderless
groups. According to the model proposed by Gerlach
and Hine (1970, 1973:163), however, a social
movement is a "group of people who are organized
for, ideologically motivated by, and committed to
a purpose which implements some form of personal
or social change, who are actively engaged in the
recruitment of others, and whose influence spreads
in opposition to the established order within which
it originated." 2

Gerlach and Hine (1970) contend, however, that
movements are not just reactions to stress caused
by a changing society, but are also mechanisms of
change which help generate the very conditions
that foster the movement's continued growth (e.g.,
when a movement's ideology leads participants to
perceive even greater opposition from the established order than already exists). Gerlach and

5

Hine (1970:xvi-ii) propose, therefore, that a
movement can "take-off" and spread into groups
even where the generating conditions do not exist
when five key factors are present and interacting:
(1) a segmented, usually decentralized cellular
organization composed of units linked by various
personal, structural, and ideological ties; (2) face-
to-face recruitment which exploits pre-existing
significant social relationships; (3) personal
commitment generated by an act or experience which
separates participants in some significant way from
the established order (or their previous place in
it), identifies them with a new set of values, and
commits them to changed patterns of behavior;
(4) a change-oriented and action-motivating ideology;
and (5) real or imagined opposition from the larger
society or some segment of the established order.

Gerlach and Hine's five-factor model was derived
from cross-cultural field research on several
social movements--the Neo-Pentecostal, Black Power,
and Conservation/Ecology Movements--and through an
examination of the available literature on a number
of other movements such as Mau Mau, early Christianity
and Islam, Communism, the student and New Left
Movements, etc. The model represents a working
hypothesis which they have found useful in understanding and analyzing this wide range of social
movements. It combines the traditional social-
psychological perspective which focused on internal
movement characteristics (cf. Smelser, 1963) with
the current interest in the impact of external
events and resources on collective behavior which
has come to be called the "resource mobilization
perspective" (Barkan, 1979:19-20; McCarthy & Zald,
1978).

The form and dynamics of the Welfare Mothers Movement in Minnesota and around the nation largely
confirms the utility of the Gerlach-Hine model.
Two modifications in the model must be made, however.
First, Gerlach and Hine's fifth factor of opposition
focuses on the inevitable conflict movements generate with at least some segments of the established
order. In order to deal more concisely and compre-
hensively with the impact of external events on the

6

success or failure of movement groups, however, this fifth factor of opposition will be expanded to include the process of gathering support for movement activities (which Gerlach and Hine discuss as a part of movement organization under "extra-movement linkages").

Second, and most important, the material collected on recruitment to Welfare Mothers Movement groups does not match the recruitment process Gerlach and Hine observed in other social movements. While not denying the power of an idea in motivating individuals to join a social movement, Gerlach and Hine (1970:79) found that an individual first became involved through a significant, pre-existing relationship with someone already in a movement group-- a relative, close friend, neighbor, or influential associate of some sort. Analysis of the recruitment of welfare mothers in Minnesota, however, suggested that while a small handful of women did initially form the core of new groups, the vast majority of members were not recruited along the lines of significant pre-existing relationships. The major cause for this variant recruitment pattern seems to be the lack of any traditional basis for solidarity among welfare mothers.

The Historical and Political Context

The ongoing relationship between local groups and national institutions or events is an important social process which social scientists must investigate in order to understand the activities not only of the poor, but of all segments of the American people. As Jenkins (1979:223) points out, Piven and Cloward (1971:147-8) have argued that the poor historically have lacked interest group organizations or the control of financial and other resources required for participating in our conventional political system. The emergence of poor people's organizations such as Welfare Mothers Movement groups, therefore, suggests that economic and political elites, particularly on the national level, must have become more vulnerable to pressure from the poor. Piven and Cloward

7

(1971:329) have identified the migration of large numbers of blacks to the cities, the Civil Rights Movement, and the ghetto rioting of the early 1960s as the events which forced the government to enact ghetto-placating federal programs and declare a War on Poverty:

> In many respects, the emergence of the National Welfare Rights Organization [and other Welfare Mothers Movement groups] represents the most striking example one could give of the federal role in stimulating the welfare explosion. For what must be recognized is that the welfare poor came to form a coherent organization as a consequence of federal intervention in the cities--as a consequence of the Great Society social workers and VISTA volunteers who became the organizers of NWRO groups, of Great Society lawyers who brought NWRO legal suits, and of the Great Society rhetoric and protection that made attacks on local welfare agencies first imaginable and then feasible.

A host of new rules designed to make relief benefits more difficult to obtain and the withdrawal of support for political protest by the poor began to take shape in the early 1970s during the Nixon administration, however (Piven & Cloward, 1973:340). The succeeding Ford administration also identified Welfare expenditures as a major cause of inflation and therefore of the urban crisis. Indeed it was difficult to find many voices in either political party which significantly disagreed about the need to cut back on welfare expenditures (Ginsberg, 1976: 38-40). This opposition had a definite chilling effect on the activities of Welfare Mothers Movement groups. By 1974 national-level coordination of the movement through NWRO had ceased. Other policies such as revenue sharing hastened the reorientation of movement groups from the national level, where resources and support were decreasing and opposition increasing, to the local level. This was reflected by a retrenchment of existing Welfare Mothers Movement groups and a renewed interest in local issues of more immediate concern to most welfare mothers.

8

As Gerlach and Hine (1973:184) suggest, however, "As a kite flies against the wind, so a movement also grows with the strength of its opposition." The part opposition plays in raising the commitment level of participants and serving as a force against which to unite a movement's disparate segments is a crucial fact of movement dynamics, and a powerful tool in the hands of those who understand it consciously or intuitively. In other words, movements among the poor appear to require not only that resources be made available to them in order for protest activities to emerge, but also an optimum level of opposition. No opposition whatsoever inhibits the spread of a movement as effectively as its suppression through the use or threat of force (Gerlach & Hine, 1970:188-9).

Field Site and Informants

The field research on which this study is based took place between 1969 and 1972 with the most intensive work done between July 1970 and July 1971. The primary research site was in Minneapolis, Minnesota although a wide range of contacts between these groups and other state-and national-level organizations were also investigated on a less intensive scale, particularly in the neighboring city of St. Paul. During this period the actions and interactions of four major groups were investigated, including early local groups such as (1) the AFDC League and (2) Direct Action Recipients of Welfare, (3) a state affiliate of the National Welfare Rights Organization, and finally (4) a new and again locally-oriented group called the Minnesota Recipients Alliance.

Research techniques included informal interviews, participant observation at the organization meetings, demonstrations, and social events of Welfare Mothers Movement groups as well as opposition groups, and the use of questionnaires. Interviews in the welfare mothers' homes proved an important source of information. For example, although I attended a few meetings of neighborhood AFDC League groups, most of my information on the AFDC League and Direct

9

Action Recipients of Welfare necessarily had to come from interviews because the organizations were in effect no longer functioning during the fieldwork period. Active members of the Minnesota Welfare Rights Organization were also interviewed using the same broad, open-ended questions with which most respondents seemed comfortable.

At the time of my research, the Welfare Mothers Movement in Minnesota was composed of a core of some 40 people. In the course of fieldwork each of the 19 major informants from MWRO, the 15 participants from the AFDC League, and two key informants from Direct Action Recipients of Welfare were interviewed at least twice. The first interview covered the organization's history, goals, and the individual's recruitment and participation with the group. The second longer interview dealt with politics, such as the conduct of meetings, leadership, sources of conflict and its resolution, and the relationship between staff and members.

A short, self-administered questionnaire was also mailed to members of the two major groups within the state--the AFDC League and MWRO. This questionnaire covered the same basic material as was raised in the interviews. Fifty-two percent of the AFDC League questionnaires were returned from participants around the state; of the MWRO questionnaires, twenty-three percent were returned.

To complement the study of the movement from the perspective of the welfare mothers themselves, interviews and informal discussions were held with four non-recipients most closely associated with the AFDC League and MWRO. In addition, interviews with officials in the welfare department, local and national politicians, and other public figures who were involved in Welfare Mothers Movement activities were also conducted in order to determine how both opponents and supporters perceived the goals, organization, and tactics of the various movement groups. A separate questionnaire was also mailed to the members of three specific groups in the larger society who had frequent contact with the movement, in order to get their reactions to recent movement

activities. These three groups were the employees
of the Hennepin County (Minneapolis) Welfare Department, members of the welfare subcommittees of the
state legislature, and the Hennepin County School
Board.

Informants were generally helpful and candid during
interviews and participant observation of movement
events, with only a few exceptions. For example,
one high-level administrator of the county welfare
department persisted in dealing with me as an advocate for Welfare Mothers Movement groups, rather
than as an independent investigator. Rapport with
recipients was aided in particular by the similarity
in my sex and age to that of the welfare mothers.
In addition, since Minneapolis had no history of
racial difficulties, contacts with black recipients
posed few, if any, problems.

It has become commonplace to point out that field
research (in "exotic" non-Western settings as well
as urban areas in our own society) is a unique human
experience. In all such human interactions, people's
motives are varied and complex. Thus the welfare
mothers understood that as a student I was interested
in learning about their organizations and activities
as part of the requirements for my education. Many
were very supportive of my involvement in their
organization for this reason alone. Most also hoped
that my research would help tell what Welfare Mothers
Movement groups were "really all about," as one
woman put it. This kind of access to publicity is
ordinarily difficult for people with little economic or political influence and so they saw possible
publication of my research findings as a positive
benefit for themselves as well. I also provided
needed transportation for many women, supported
fund-raising efforts, and was able to pay key informants a nominal sum for their second interviews
through a special research grant from the Anthropology
Department of the University of Minnesota.

Inevitably my presence occasionally had an impact
on the internal politics of ongoing movement organizations, such as MWRO. For example, during meetings
I ordinarily took notes on what was happening. On

11

a few occasions, welfare mothers approached me to
find out "what had really happened" at a meeting
(i.e., what decisions had been made or if a vote
had really been taken) when there was a dispute over
an issue within the group. On other occasions I
was a pawn in the power struggle between some of
the leaders of MWRO and staff members. My presence
at a sensitive meeting, then, was sometimes requested
by leaders who wished to assert their control over
the organization in opposition to the organizers
who attempted to keep me from attending meetings in
which there might be a lot of internal conflict or
"dirty linen" aired. Some, although not all, of
these staff members resented my involvement with
MWRO because they were suspicious of my motives and
the ultimate uses to which the material from my
study might be put. From an outsider's point of
view, however, some of their opposition stemmed
from an attempt to limit the welfare mothers' contacts with non-recipients (as will be discussed in
more detail in Chapter Seven in the section on
"Intermediaries"). As a result, interviews with
one organizer were initially very difficult to set
up, but by the end of the research period much of
her hostility had disappeared.

In general, my orientation in this field research
was not as a statistician but as an observer.
Eames and Goode (1973:5) suggest that the essence
of the anthropological framework is, in fact, a
descriptive, humanist approach, the use of the
culture concept (modified to accurately reflect the
nature of complex societies), and the relativist
position that cultural systems cannot be comparative-
ly evaluated as better or worse than others. The
discipline's traditional emphasis on cultural rela-
tivity is particularly critical for research conducted
on one's own culture. Studying groups in our own
society who are "urbanized" or "acculturated," who
have a material culture which is not foreign, who
live in physical settings with which we are familiar
and who speak the same language, makes it all too
easy for researchers to approach such groups with
preconceived categories and to assume they understand the motives and meanings of people's actions
(Guillemin, 1975:303). Anthropologists of course,

12

are largely children of the suburban middle class just as are other social scientists and bureaucrats who deal with the poor. Guillemin (1975:306-7) suggests the answer to this dilemma lies in knowing your own personal limits to interclass contact, in exploring the ways in which "our world" is institutionally connected to theirs, and in taking on the role of the stranger (i.e., ethnographer) in another community.

For these reasons the traditional anthropological techniques of participant observation and open-ended interviewing were selected as most appropriate. Questionnaires were formulated and distributed only after a working knowledge of the movement had been acquired and the women's confidence gained. Selection of a random sample of welfare mothers from movement groups was not feasible due to the nature of the research situation.[3] Membership lists were not well kept in many groups and members moved frequently. In addition, women who knew me or about my project from a mutual friend were receptive and cooperative, but complete strangers occasionally were reticent about discussing their participation in movement groups. For example, despite assurances of anonymity, some women expressed fear about the possibility of reprisals from the welfare department or harassment from members of the general public if their participation in a movement group became widely known. Occasionally a woman would refuse to talk to me because she was no longer on welfare and did not wish her current neighbors and friends to know she had previously received public assistance.

Beyond the core of key informants whom I interviewed intensively and with whom I developed ties of friendship, a great many other welfare mothers and outsiders also contributed a good deal of information. Some of the best opportunities for discussing movement activities and women's perception of events occurred while driving welfare mothers to or from meetings, or during the long hours of a demonstration. Contact with national-level NWRO members and staff took place during their occasional trips to Minneapolis and during the summer of 1971 at the NWRO Convention in Providence, R.I.

Approximately 100 people were the informants from whom specific material was obtained for this study. The fullest information was collected from and about the welfare mothers involved in movement groups in Minnesota; more limited material was collected, for comparative purposes, from outsiders who were both friends and opponents of various movement groups.

Description and Analysis

As Piven and Cloward (1977:266) point out, "Virtually nothing has been written about NWRO," much less about other Welfare Mothers Movement groups. Even during the height of Welfare Mothers Movement activity, groups received relatively little support from other movements and have since been paid scant attention by historians or social scientists.[4] In addition, with the exception of Steiner (1971), most research on the movement has been conducted by students inspired by Piven and Cloward's (1971, 1977) approach.

While this study also has benefited greatly from Piven and Cloward's (1971) early work detailing the historical and economic forces which influence the behavior of the poor, it contests a major point in their latest analysis. As Jenkins (1979:223)states:

> Piven and Cloward's main challenge is to those who advocate the organization of permanent, membership-based associations among the poor . . . and to the Alinsky "school" of community organizing. To Alinsky's dictim, "if you want drama get a movement; if you want results, get an organization," Piven and Cloward argue, ". . . it is not possible to compel concessions from elites or sustain oppositional organizations over time. . . . Insurgency is always short-lived. . . . Whatever the people win is a response to their turbulence and not to their organized numbers."

Piven and Cloward, in other words, argue that "movements" and "organizations" are inherently antithetical. Their view, moreover, assumes the only

14

options open to movements are to develop a bureaucratic organization or to remain a loose-knit cadre
of organizers (the latter of which they prefer).

The model put forward by Gerlach and Hine (1970,
1973), on the other hand, hypothesizes that movements are by their nature complex, polycentric,
largely informally structured operations, not fixed
hierarchies with rigid rules (Jenkins, 1979:226).
Gerlach and Hine (1970:33) argue that it is in fact,
precisely our cultural assumption that "organizations"
must have a clear-cut leadership and a pyramidal,
hierarchical structure which has hindered social
scientists' understanding of movement dynamics.
Only recently have researchers begun to look into
the impact which organizational forms have on the
selection of goals and tactics by social movements
(cf. Barkan, 1979; Gamson, 1975).

The Gerlach and Hine approach, therefore, would
appear to be a particularly useful analytical and
descriptive tool for a study of the Welfare Mothers
Movement. While providing a useful corrective to
an ethnocentric perception of the organization of
movements, it also broadens the definition of the
research unit. Whereas Piven and Cloward focus
exclusively on NWRO (and particularly on WRO activities on the East Coast), the Gerlach-Hine model
emphasizes the linkages between all groups on the
local and national level. Extension of analysis
and description to include this broader range of
groups suggests that this was truly a "Welfare
Mothers Movement" and not exclusively a "Welfare
Rights Movement," as Piven and Cloward have labelled
it. The material from the movement in Minnesota
not only adds to the literature on the Welfare
Mothers Movement, but widens its geographical range
and provides a longer time frame by including movement groups which both preceded and succeeded
national-level coordination through NWRO.

Finally, one of the most common problems in the lit-
eratur on poverty results from the failure to
delineate the different factors influencing the
behavior of the poor--to the careless equation between factors due to poverty or class, to racism and

15

ethnicity, to different age groups, and to sex roles (Eames & Goode, 1973:12). Piven and Cloward (1979:x) analyze the Welfare Mothers Movement primarily as an expression of class conflict. Their attention to class variables, however, has led to a neglect of the impact of traditional female gender roles on the opportunities and constraints experienced by groups of welfare mothers. The perspective used in this study, therefore, provides a challenge to the widely accepted notion that class position is the sole cause of the subordination and effective disenfranchisement of welfare mothers in America.

The second chapter in this book describes the historical development of both our attitudes toward poverty in general and our contemporary welfare system in particular. In addition, an outline of the major functions of the national, state, and local levels of the public welfare system gives a brief look at an institution which is not a familiar one to most Americans. Such an understanding is vital to an analysis of the Welfare Mothers Movement, for it was largely in reaction to the welfare system that much of the ideology, goals, and tactics of movement groups developed.

Chapter Three is primarily a description of the local history of the movement in Minnesota and gives a chronological survey of the political activities of the four main groups which emerged in the state between 1964 and 1973. At the same time, an account of local and national events which were closely linked to the expansion and contraction of the movement during that decade are outlined.

Chapters Four through Seven analyze the Welfare Mothers Movement in terms of Gerlach and Hine's five factors of movement dynamics: organization, ideology, recruitment and commitment, and opposition and support.

The last chapter not only summarizes the main findings of my research, but also addresses itself to the issues raised here: (1) how a broader perspective on the movement as a whole effects our judgment about the success or failure of the Welfare Mothers Movement, and (2) the relationship of this movement to the Women's Liberation Movement and the feminist perspective in general. An appreciation of these issues will enable us to determine to what degree this was indeed a decade of change.

FOOTNOTES

1. As Wolf (1968:16-17) describes them, patron-client ties are characterized by a minimum of affect, multiplex relationships, and a differential capacity to grant goods and services. In the relationship, the patron provides economic aid and protection which the client pays back largely in more intangible assets, such as demonstrations of esteem and loyalty, information on the activities of others, and the promise of political support.

2. Gerlach and Hine's definition would be too narrow to encompass either movements that are attempting to defend the established order against change (e.g., the Moral Majority) or movements that concentrate on changing individual participants while being relatively indifferent to the larger society (e.g. communal religious movements or E.S.T.). The definition is adequate, however, for the purposes of this study of the Welfare Mothers Movement.

3. Although a random sample could not be obtained, an attempt was made to interview all members from two types of groups. The welfare mothers involved in the AFDC League and MWRO were divided between those who lived in public housing projects and those who lived in private low-cost housing scattered throughout the city. One group (from each of these two major organizations) which was composed of project residents and one group from each whose members were scattered throughout a larger neighborhood were interviewed. No major differences were found between these two groups in terms of the women's personal histories, their reason for participation or length of membership. The material was combined, therefore, and treated together in the analysis.

4. See for example the largely unpublished studies by Gelb and Sardell, 1973; Kurzman, 1971; Martin, 1972; Rothman, 1969; and Whittaker, 1970.

CHAPTER 2

The Institutional Context: The Welfare System

The administration of welfare inevitably is influenced by our attitudes toward poverty. A brief
review of the source of these attitudes and the
historical development of our relief practices will
enable us to comprehend more fully the operation of
the present welfare system. As Parker (1973:271)
points out:

> Many different societies have been aware of
> poverty. Various are the explanations of pov-
> erty which have been offered. In preindustrial
> Europe, poverty, though regarded as unfortunate
> was considered one of the mysterious workings
> of God and was, in fact, imbued with an aura of
> holiness and moral purity. . . With the emergence
> of the bourgeoisie and the Industrial Revolution,
> this earlier view was altered. In the conflict
> that ensued between the rising middle class and
> the old aristocracy, a new view of humanity was
> required. The newly acquired good fortune of
> the merchants, traders, and early factory owners
> was explained on the grounds of personal merit
> and hard work. The obverse of this coin was
> that poverty must be due to personal or moral
> defects.

Thus Western relief systems developed during the
long, difficult transition from feudalism to capitalism in a social environment which had become
critical of poverty. Between 1500 and 1850, cycles
of population explosion and agricultural dislocations
among people not yet fully incorporated into the
industrial system caused widespread disruption and
poverty. One of the earliest attempts to deal with
this problem came in 1572 when the Elizabethan Poor
Law was formulated to provide a local tax for the
support of paupers. The distribution of this money
was to be overseen by the local justices of the peace
and in many ways paupers were treated much as petty
criminals throughout the period. The practice of
taking men from their families for periods in the
workhouse and the indenture of women and children
from impoverished families also developed at this

time, due in large part to the needs of the developing industrial labor system (Piven & Cloward, 1971:8-15, 24-31). It is from this Poor Law heritage that many of our underlying cultural attitudes towards the dependent poor have come.

Poverty in America

The social history of the United States is often described in terms of poor immigrants coming to this country and working their way up toward security and success. Although studies suggest that upward mobility was not as great as popularly assumed, many families did include some relative who came with little and worked their way up, if not far up (Leacock, 1971:17). American thinking about poverty, however, has been greatly influenced both by a belief in the morality of hard work and by the assumption that the equality of opportunity found in America provided a chance for at least moderate success for all people. We tend to believe, therefore, that if a person is really poor it must be because he or she does not work hard enough, or worse, does not want to work at all (Garretson, 1976b:48).

In spite of these beliefs, some financial aid was provided for the poor in the United States prior to this century through the efforts of private charities. By the 1930s, however, the role of private philanthropic organizations had changed due in large part to the effects of the Great Depression on the amount of charitable giving. The influence of psychoanalytic theory also hastened the reorientation of these groups from the giving of financial aid to the provision of psychological or social services (Klein, 1968:148-58). A number of state-level public assistance programs began to be developed in the first several decades of the 20th century in order to fill the gap left by the inability of many private philanthropies to provide financial aid (Handler, 1972:11-12).

The Depression. This period saw the growth of large numbers of unemployed and dislocated Americans and disruptions at state relief offices. According to

20

Piven and Cloward (1971:64-76), as a result of these
pressures the Roosevelt administration pushed through
several federal programs to rescue the over-burdened
state public assistance programs and to provide
work and/or direct relief to the poor. Thus, as
Steiner (1971:6) points out, the basic skeleton of
the present public welfare system dates from the
era of the New Deal. The system is based on the
development of a centralized federal-state program
to provide financial support as well as public housing, surplus commodity distribution and food stamps,
public employment for the poor, and special youth
programs. Since this era, however, our welfare
programs have grown by gradual accretion, rather
than as the result of a unified social welfare plan.

The 1940s and 1950s. As the administration of the
public welfare laws became more professionalized,
the federal government attempted to set minimum
standards for the welfare field. This was to be
accomplished through federally-funded state programs
of public assistance in the areas of Aid to Dependent
Children, Aid to the Disabled, Aid to the Blind,
and Old Age Assistance. In other words, the granting of federal monies was made contingent upon the
acceptance of federal standards for welfare administration (Handler, 1972:15). During this time a
number of important principles were developed
(although not always put into practice in all
states). For example, the confidentiality of records
was established, while the practice of holding relatives responsible for contributing to the support
of those on public assistance and the surrender of
property in exchange for relief were discouraged.

Despite the growth in federal control of welfare
programs which is characteristic of this period,
the states still remained primarily responsible for
the administration of the programs. Often these
federal standards amounted primarily to symbolic
gestures; states and communities which wished to
could find loopholes in the law to avoid changing
actual administrative practices. In addition,
since the programs were still state-run, there continued to be a great deal of variety among the
states as to eligibility, benefits, and other conditions for receiving welfare (Handler, 1972:58).

During this period the AFDC rolls continued to expand, going up by 17% in the 1950s (Piven & Cloward, 1971:183). Social and economic factors, such as increased industrialization and specialization (which decreased the availability of jobs to the unskilled), periodic recessions, a national rise in divorce and desertion rates, and a rising cost of living were major factors involved in the growth of the welfare rolls (Burgess & Price, 1963:191).

The Great Society. In the 1960s, however, three major, interrelated events occurred. First, there was an AFDC "explosion" in all regions of the country and in both rural and urban areas. Welfare went up by 31% in the first four years of the decade and by another 58% between 1964 and 1968. Second, this coincided with widespread urban disorders among blacks, including Civil Rights demonstrations and riots in the ghetto. Third, a series of anti-poverty measures were proposed by the Johnson administration in 1964 in order to build a Great Society. Most notable was the establishment of the Office of Economic Opportunity (OEO) and the development of the policy of "maximum feasible participation" by the poor (Piven & Cloward, 1971:145-50).

Great Society programs, although they may never have been intended to, put real pressure on local governments through: (1) the dissemination of information to the poor about the availability of welfare; (2) litigation which challenged a host of local laws and policies; and (3) indirect support of grass-roots organizations of the poor. For example, welfare litigation struck down a number of regulations which had kept the needy off the relief rolls. Residence laws which denied aid to welfare recipients who moved across state lines and "man-in-the-house" rules were declared illegal. Suits successfully challenged administrative procedures such as arbitrary termination of cases and mass searches without warrants (the notorious "midnight raids"). Recipients were given the right to a trial-like hearing with constitutional safeguards and the presence of a "third-party" (whether friend, lawyer, or welfare rights advocate) if so desired (Piven & Cloward, 1971:306-14). Handler (1972:74-6) points out, however, that:

22

Although there is considerable debate about how much each of these factors contributed to the growth of the AFDC program, the fact remains that the rate of growth was staggering during the decade. . . . Pressure was growing not only to relieve the financial burdens of the states, but to solve the two major inequities of AFDC: the unequal treatment of welfare families between various states and the disparity between welfare families and working-poor families.

The Nixon Family Assistance Plan. In 1969 two welfare reforms, which had been in the planning stage for some time, were finally implemented: (1) the development of citizen advisory councils in all local and state welfare departments was required; and (2) the separation of services and payments occurred. This latter reform meant that the giving of financial aid could no longer be made conditional upon the acceptance of social services, such as counseling or advice on budgeting and marketing (Walz, 1970).

In addition, President Nixon proposed a more complete reform of the welfare system in the summer of 1969. His Family Assistance Plan (FAP) represented in some respects a departure from the welfare system outlined in the previous paragraphs. According to Hoshino (1970:157), FAP had three major components: (1) a guaranteed annual income (which would be a wage supplement to the working poor) to bring all families of four up to $1600/year plus $850 of foodstamps; (2) the provision of psychological and social services; and (3) an elaborate system of work incentives, including registration for work or job training by all able-bodied adults except the mothers of pre-school age children. Despite the new concept of a guaranteed income, however, Hoshino suggests that the underlying premise of Nixon's plan reflected the moralistic philosophy of our Poor Law heritage by emphasizing the poor individual's presumed shortcomings (e.g., improper socialization in the work ethic, loafing, etc.), not the societal and economic causes of poverty.

By this combination of elements into a single piece of legislation, Nixon set the stage for the rejection of FAP by Congress. Liberals and organizations of the poor applauded the concept of a guaranteed annual income, but felt the amount proposed was not adequate and rejected the forced work provisions of the bill. Conservatives on the other hand, felt it was too generous because "people should be dissatisfied with welfare, and the more dissatisfied the better" (ABC, 1971). At the time of my research, therefore, the United States had essentially the same public welfare system whose history has been traced above.

The Structure of the Welfare System

The public welfare system is composed of sets of relationships between governmental and administrative bodies on the national, state, and county levels. The three levels are linked by policy-making, supervisory, funding, and administrative activities. with some exceptions, the federal-state-locality nexus has been characterized as one of decreasing liberality and increasing discretion. As Elman (1966:18-20) describes it:

> The various federal statutes by which people qualify for public assistance. . . have been made operative under state welfare codes, which tend to be even more restrictive in attempting to define and determine needs; and then have been placed . . . under the administration of state and local functionaries who are jealous of their prerogatives, anxious to use discretion, and subject to greater political pressures from their local communities than from the generally benign federal establishment. A veteran welfare worker gave me as a rule of thumb of Welfare administration that "the Feds propose, the states oppose, and the localities dispose" of new programs.

Each of these three levels have specific tasks, however, which they ideally must perform in accordance with the welfare statutes.

Federal/state relations. The relationship between the Department of Health, Education, and Welfare

(now the Department of Health and Human Services)
and the Minnesota Department of Public Welfare con-
sists largely of a flow of policies, supervision,
and financial resources down to the state. As the
Public Welfare Manual of the state of Minnesota (1957:
part II, section 1000) indicates, "Public welfare
in Minnesota is locally administered and state
supervised, yet as the state central agency, the
Department of Public Welfare must conform to certain
legal requirements of the Department of Health,
Education, and Welfare" (HEW).

Although formally at the top of the hierarchy, however, HEW often is dependent upon the states and
localities for an upward flow of the information it
needs to perform its supervisory functions. Furthermore, while HEW has often threatened the withdrawal
of funding to states which are not in conformity
with federal regulations, it has always backed down;
the agency has not cut off any state's funds since
1938 (Handler, 1972:61).

State/county relations. In Minnesota, state-county
relations involve not only the welfare departments
on these two levels, but also a body of elected
officials, the county welfare boards.

> The Minnesota Department of Public Welfare (DPW)
> is the State Agency responsible under a number
> of statutes for the administration of various
> financial aid and service programs. As such,
> it is responsible for giving guidance to county
> agencies, channeling information and exchanging
> experiences between county agencies, developing
> policies and procedures, and requiring practices
> that will make the various welfare laws and
> their programs as uniformly administered and as
> beneficial as possible to the recipients who are
> in need of the aids and services provided.
>
> The county welfare boards in most instances
> render the actual services and are, therefore,
> responsible for furnishing the materials and
> substance from which the public welfare programs
> are planned and formulated, through both the
> State Agency and legislature. (The State of
> Minnesota, 1957:I-1000)

In other words, policy-making and supervision in the state/county relationship are to move down. Appeals of county decisions and a flow of information about how state policies are affecting local welfare conditions move upward. This is accomplished through testimony given at public hearings and through both formal and informal communication channels within the welfare bureaucracy. The county welfare boards, however, wield a great deal of power because they control the purse strings. Without the board's approval, programs cannot be implemented. Figure 1 shows the formal organization chart of the public welfare system as it existed during the time of this study.

<u>Clients and the county welfare system</u>. Until the late 1960s, the client's only direct contact with the welfare system was through her social worker. While there are always "good" social workers and helpful administrators, the average recipient knows little about the operation of the welfare system and is therefore dependent on the competency and discretion of her worker. Many clients are not aware of review procedures which are available to them or are fearful of making use of them.

An attempt was made to remedy this situation by developing a structured setting for communication between the welfare department and its recipients. In 1969, as a result of a federal directive, citizen's advisory committees were established on the state and county levels. One-third of the members of these advisory committees were to be recipients from all categories of public assistance (including both representatives of organized groups and some unaffiliated recipients) with the remaining two-thirds to be drawn from other interested community organizations.

Welfare in Minnesota

Each state differs somewhat in the ways in which it interprets and implements the regulations and directives it receives from higher levels of the welfare bureaucracy. Such differences can substantially affect the experience of welfare. A brief

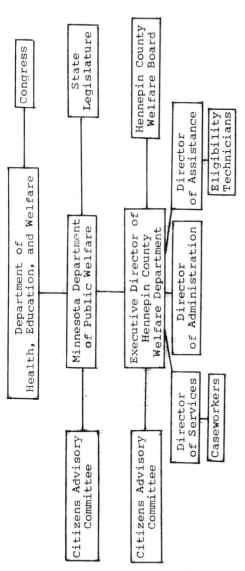

Figure 1. Organizational Chart of the State of Minnesota Welfare System (1971)

review of some of the special features of the welfare
system in Minnesota will provide a background for
the description of the history of the Welfare Mothers
Movement in Chapter Three.

In Minnesota, the state Commissioner of Welfare and
the Department of Public Welfare have consistently
acted as a liberalizing force vis-a-vis a rural-
dominated and frequently financially conservative
state legislature. As a result of the welfare system's efforts to increase welfare benefits, Minnesota
ranked fourth in the nation in the level of financial
assistance at the time of my field research. As one
welfare administrator put it, the social work community of the state felt itself to have a "proud record
of progressive administration."

As an example of this progressive approach, the director of the AFDC program on the state level pointed
out that an informal advisory board had been established on his own initiative two years before the
federal directive in this regard. Although this
advisory board was designed to encourage an exchange
of information with the organized welfare mothers
in the state, it did not work out as well in practice as was originally hoped, as the following
interview with the state Commissioner of Welfare
suggests:

Hertz: What role does the advisory committee have
         in influencing decision-making within the
         welfare department?

Commissioner: Well, [I listen to] whatever advice
         they want to give me on legislation, policy,
         budgets. They recommended for example, a law
         to get legal assistance for the poor.

Hertz: Can you give me an estimate of how often
         their advice is really enacted into some kind
         of policy?

Commissioner: I don't know. We went over this pro-
         posed flat grant with them, I'm sure. Well,
         I'm not sure. Anyway the system wasn't enacted
         as policy by the department so whatever their
         advice was, it didn't make any difference. . . .

We had to bring up most of the points for discussion, anyway. Their chief recommendations
are always that they get more money--you can't
discuss that for too many meetings.

While the AFDC League had earlier had several women
attending the state-level advisory committee, by the
time of my research none of the Welfare Mothers Movement groups had a representative on the committee,
in spite of several attempts by the DPW to find new
members. In contrast, militant groups actively sought
a place on the county advisory committee. Observation of several committee meetings in 1971, however,
suggested that it also had little impact on the form-
ulation of welfare policy. Although the committee's
stated function was to advise the county welfare
board, it had no funds with which to conduct its own
research or planning. It was, therefore, never in
a position to be independent, assertive, or innova-
tive in its suggestions, and ended up resignedly
rubber-stamping departmental proposals and actions.

Finally, the relationship between the state- and
county-level welfare systems was also generally an
amicable and cooperative one--with the possible exception of that between the Department of Public
Welfare and the Hennepin County (Minneapolis) Welfare
Department. This relationship was an important
feature of the institutional context within which
the Welfare Mothers Movement in Minnesota developed,
for it was in Minneapolis that the most active and
long-lived movement organizations appeared. One
informant described the relationship in this way:

[There is] a bias on the part of the Commissioner
and the whole Department of Public Welfare
against Hennepin County. They see Hennepin
County as giving out nearly 63% of all supple-
mental grants in the State of Minnesota.
Hennepin County has between 25 and 30% of all
recipients and the highest standard level of
assistance for the state. They give out special
grants without batting an eye. Telephone, newspaper, and non-medical transportation are
specials according to the state, but a matter
of course here. I don't like to take many
appeals for Hennepin County recipients because
generally they're going to lose.

Thus the Hennepin County Welfare Department differed from the generalization made above that localities tend to be more financially restrictive than higher levels of the welfare system.

In summary, the welfare system in the United States has its historical roots in the punitive practices of the Elizabethan Poor Law. There has been a great deal of progress in changing the practices inherited from this tradition over the last forty years as a result of the efforts of social work professionals and the federal government, as well as welfare recipients. Where discretion on the part of local welfare departments is allowed, however, some demeaning practices may continue. This is due largely to many Americans' negative judgments and attitudes toward the dependent poor, particularly those receiving AFDC (Handler, 1972:1-3). Thus, as Cloward and Elman (1966) have indicated, much of the strategy of the poor has been to organize, to define their receipt of financial assistance as a "right" rather than a "charity," to get information about these rights, and to demonstrate that their rights can be successfully asserted in the face of opposition from significant segments of the larger society.

CHAPTER 3

The History of the Welfare Mothers Movement

Until the last several years, there was a tendency
in the social science literature to analyze the behavior of the poor as if they were isolated from
the impact of urban and national institutions and
events. The presumed autonomy and distinctiveness
of people living in the ghettos, barrios, and reser-
vations of the United States was particularly characteristic of the culture of poverty approach originally formulated by Lewis (1966). Neglect of external forces was also found, albeit to a lesser
extent, even in the early poverty studies which
emphasized the situational factors affecting the
values and behavior of the poor (e.g., Liebow,
1968). While focusing exclusively on a poor, racial,
or ethnic community provides a neat and manageable
unit for research purposes, such a strategy does not
do justice to the economic and political interde-
pendencies which link all segments of our society
together (Jones, 1972:51-2).

The poor are not isolated from the larger society.
A number of recent studies have suggested in fact
that organizations of the poor of all races and
ethnic groups are especially vulnerable to the actions
of political and economic elites (cf. Hertz, 1978;
Jones, 1972; McFee, 1972; Spicer, 1970). This
historical sketch of the Welfare Mothers Movement
in Minnesota, therefore, includes an account of the
events on the local and national levels which were
most closely linked to the expansion and contraction
of the movement during the decade between the mid-
1960s and the mid-1970s.

In the early 1960s, a number of small, neighborhood
groups of welfare mothers were formed, particularly
in the two largest cities in Minnesota--Minneapolis
and St. Paul. These social clubs were formed largely
as a result of the activities of social workers in
local community centers who believed that welfare
mothers would benefit from an opportunity to social-
ize and discuss their welfare and personal problems
together.

31

Between 1964 and 1972, however, several larger organizations appeared which differed from these earlier clubs. The key element which distinguishes these later organizations was a commitment to the idea that welfare mothers must organize themselves in order to achieve a measure of political influence on the institutions most directly affecting their lives. The principal groups within the Welfare Mothers Movement in Minnesota were: (1) the AFDC (Aid to Families with Dependent Children) League; (2) Direct Action Recipients of Welfare; (3) a local branch of the National Welfare Rights Organization which was called the Minnesota Welfare Rights Organization (MWRO); and (4) the Minnesota Recipients Alliance (see Figure 2). These four groups, although they developed sequentially and occasionally competed with each other for followers and financial support, were linked together through overlapping membership, a core of shared beliefs, and short-term alliances into a social movement.

The AFDC League

All informants agreed on the basic details of the founding of the AFDC League, but the versions differed in emphasis on some points. As Wheeldon (1970:143) found in her study of the history of Coloured voluntary associations in South Africa, such differences result primarily from the way in which the activities, motivations, and capabilities of the subordinate group are perceived by different segments of the society. Differing versions of the founding of community organizations are not due primarily to idiosyncratic variation, therefore, but serve to reinforce the stereotype each group has about the other's proper role in society.

In accounts of the founding of the AFDC League, the amount of initiative displayed by the recipients as opposed to members of the social work community differed. The following version, told to me by one of the founders of the AFDC League, Edna Eberly, is representative of the recipient's perception of events. (To protect the anonymity of informants, all names used in the text are pseudonyms.)

At the beginning, everybody was against us

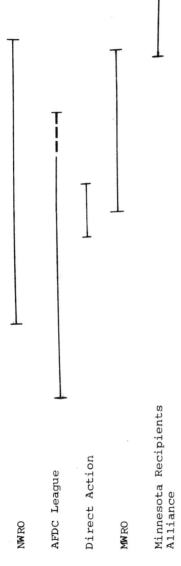

Figure 2. Time-span of Welfare Mothers Movement Groups

because everybody was down on AFDC mothers
in the late 1950s and early 1960s. To admit
that you were on welfare just wasn't done.
You went about your business and tried not to
let anyone know you were getting helped. . . .
Well, one of the things that kicked this group
off was a legislator in St. Paul, who claimed
that people were trading children and getting
more benefits. Anybody with two ounces of
sense would know this is an impossibility.
We kind of wanted to refute some of those
charges. But we had no intention of starting
a group until Ramsey County [St. Paul] passed
a ruling that welfare mothers no longer had to
go to the county hospital, but could go to
private doctors--but they didn't tell the girls
about it. Then one by one we found it out. We
started comparing notes about what different
ones could and couldn't get [from their worker]
and this made Ellen very mad. She called a
meeting over in St. Paul about it--just a few
friends who were in Solo Parents [YWCA] to try
and find out why. That first night we got
together, Ellen made this broad statement that
we should go to the legislature about these
problems. A reporter picked it up, so we were
almost committed to go before we even met and
formed the AFDC League. This meeting was
reported in the St. Paul paper and a member of
the Community Health and Welfare Council in
Minneapolis called me and asked if I had gone
to the meeting. I said I hadn't, but if I
could start a group in Minneapolis, would he
come and talk to us. I strongly felt the need
for some sort of organization. I called the
YWCA and asked if it were possible to get a
room to use for this. I talked to June Waldheim,
who said she didn't think there was any reason
the YWCA couldn't do it. So then I called the
newspaper and inserted a little article in it
that there would be a meeting. . . . I think
we had 75 mothers turn out that night, including
some of those who had gotten together in St.
Paul. The man from the Community Health and
Welfare Council who attended was able to enthuse
those people we hadn't talked to personally
with the fact that we needed to band together.
We just called it a "league" and said we'd have

another meeting the following month for the specific purpose of setting up some legislative ideas on what we wanted--areas we felt needed improvement.

On the other hand, June Waldheim, the YWCA Adult Activities coordinator who eventually worked with the AFDC League for many years in an unpaid staff capacity, tended to emphasize the part played by outsiders in her response to my question about how she had come in contact with the AFDC League:

> Come in contact with it? I started it! It started back in the fall of 1964. One woman, Ellen Lasalle in St. Paul, got very perturbed over a statement about mothers exchanging children and getting double benefits. She wrote WCCO [a local television station] and asked if she and Edna Eberly could have equal time to rebut this statement. All the women were in the Solo Parents of the YWCA at the time. So then they got together and said we've got to do something about this and they turned to the YWCA because they were familiar with it. Anyway, at WCCO at this time was George Rice, who did a series of favorable editorials on AFDC. Then an interim subcommittee of the state legislature invited the women, as a result of this TV coverage, to testify before their committee. They had met a couple of times in St. Paul, so we thought we should get a couple of women together here in Minneapolis. One of the men from the Health and Welfare Council called the executive director of the YWCA and pushed us, saying that we had to do something. I had been following it and knew the people involved so we called a meeting. We only had a small paragraph in the newspaper [announcing the meeting] , but about 80 women came to this first meeting. We told them what they could accomplish as an organized group. The man from the Health and Welfare Council likened it to the situation of the retarded--for so many years they had been ashamed of their situation and it wasn't until they faced it and started doing something that there had been so much progress. . . . The women had a great deal of help

from the director of the state AFDC program and someone from the Ramsey County Welfare Department. Between them, they gave us a picture of what the laws were. You know, "If we didn't like such and such, was it an administrative or legislative problem, and if legislative, was it under the Minnesota State Legislature, and are they going along with federal laws. . ." So they gave us the background and the actual legal situation and the women at that time picked out about seven priorities.

These two versions highlight the contrasting way in which insiders and outsiders view the origins of such organizations. As Gerlach and Hine (1970) point out, however, it is the participants' perception of these events which plays an important part in the growth and spread of movement groups. The AFDC League members' understanding about the role welfare mothers played in the formation of the group was a source of pride to them, and affirmed their belief that welfare recipients were capable of taking effective action to bring about change.

Influenced by the suggestions of the welfare administrators who spoke at these early meetings, AFDC League founders drew up the following recommendations for the 1964 session of the state legislature (Hertz, 1978:139): (1) a work incentive plan; (2) continued payments to children who are past the age of 18, but who are continuing their education; (3) making residence requirements less restrictive; (4) enlarging the scope of the AFDC program to include unemployed fathers; (5) raising the equity limit on real estate holdings which can be retained by women when they went on relief; (6) abolishing township (i.e., local) relief in Minneapolis; (7) tightening up laws on the enforcement of the father's legal obligation to support his children; and (8) providing a burial allowance for welfare mothers from AFDC funds.

The women made carefully prepared, sedate presentations of these proposed changes in the welfare laws at legislative hearings. They emphasized that as welfare mothers, they knew more about welfare than most of the legislators did and so could provide important input on welfare issues. None of these recommendations was enacted into law during the 1964 session, however.

Nor did members of the welfare system and AFDC League participants attach the same importance to the various reforms. Kaplan (1966) points out that AFDC League members were particularly interested in the burial allowance issue. Under AFDC regulations, mothers who died while on the program, unlike their children, must have a burial paid from poor relief (rather than AFDC) funds. The women felt this reflected a negative attitude toward welfare mothers and so assigned this reform a higher priority on their list of legislative changes than did the professional social work community.

During this first year, the AFDC League participants in Minneapolis and St. Paul formed two county-wide groups. Officers were kept to a minimum and most activities were planned by ad hoc committees or by the top leaders. All the women's energies were focused on lobbying at the state legislature.

By the summer of 1965, however, two events led to an increased formalization of the AFDC League's structure. First, AFDC League leaders realized that the organization's goal of lobbying to change state welfare laws was temporarily frustrated by the recess of the state legislature. As the legislature meets only biennially in Minnesota, the AFDC League had a whole year in which alternative activities must be planned if the group was to avoid losing membership or disappearing altogether. Second, fledgling AFDC League organizations were beginning to appear in counties outside the Twin Cities, and the women felt these should be drawn into a statewide group. The AFDC League leaders were particularly anxious to organize these "outstate" women because they hoped they would eventually serve as an effective means of pressuring rural legislators in the next session.

During 1965 and 1966, then, AFDC League members began a concerted effort to develop a stable organization and to evolve a well-defined ideology and set of goals. According to a mimeographed brochure (AFDC League, 1966), the group's goals were:

> (1) to encourage self-improvement; (2) to work with responsible community groups and the Public Welfare Board to attack the problems of AFDC

children and their guardians; and (3) to create awareness of the responsibilities as well
as the rights of recipients.

Informants consistently stated they believed the
AFDC League had worked to bring about important
changes in the larger society. Such change, however,
could only be brought about by "playing the game"
according to the establishment's rules, as they put
it--by learning how to lobby effectively and by cul-
tivating contacts with individuals in the welfare
department and other influential community groups.

At the same time, the women admitted that at least
as much of their energy had been invested in self-
help activities designed to get themselves off the
welfare rolls through education or job training.
They felt that such self-help had an impact beyond
the individual welfare mother, however, by demonstrating the women were capable of taking the initiative
and bettering their lives. Thus, ultimately, the
negative public stereotype of the welfare recipient
would be changed.

The AFDC League presented the same set of reforms to
the state legislature again in the 1966-67 session,
lobbying along with the county and state welfare system and social work organizations such as the National
Association of Social Workers for their passage. The
major success in this session was the enactment into
law of their recommendation to permit children who
were still attending school to continue receiving
AFDC payments (although only through the age of 19).
Regardless of the degree to which the passage of this
reform was actually due to pressure from the welfare
professionals, as opposed to the efforts of the AFDC
League, most welfare mothers perceived it as a victory. Leaders of the AFDC League and nonrecipients
associated with the group, such as June Waldheim, were
quick to point out the importance of the support given
the AFDC League in its early years, however. One
of the most crucial, yet most intangible, sources of
support stemmed from the generally favorable climate
of opinion which prevailed at the time.

According to Piven and Cloward (1971:189-98), the
appearance of early Welfare Mothers Movement organizations, such as the AFDC League (and NWRO on the East

38

Coast) was preceded by a number of seemingly unrelated events, particularly the migration of blacks to the cities as the result of the modernization of Southern agriculture. These population movements and the job discrimination experienced by blacks in Northern cities combined to produce a "substantial weakening of social controls and widespread outbreaks of disorder" within the black community. The protest and urban riots of the early 1960s, along with the turmoil created by the Civil Rights Movement, led ultimately to the enactment of a series of "ghetto-placating" federal programs such as the antipoverty programs.

By-passing local governments, antipoverty workers directly stimulated demands for an increase in local services (such as welfare) by helping all those who were eligible to obtain welfare benefits. Community organizations in poor neighborhoods were formed and their leaders encouraged to become involved in politics. Thus, the philosophy of the Great Society which had stimulated the development of the antipoverty program also helped to create a climate on the local level in which a measure of direct political participation by the poor was encouraged for the first time (Piven & Cloward, 1971:274-82).

In Minnesota, this new philosophy was translated into tangible support for the early organizing efforts of the AFDC League through a sympathetic press, the liberal city government of then Mayor Naftalin, professional social work organizations, and private groups, such as the YWCA. Even most county welfare departments, particularly that of Minneapolis, were cooperative with the AFDC League.

After the close of the 1966-67 legislative session, however, meetings of the state-level (as well as many county) AFDC Leagues ceased. The few small groups which remained active began to focus on neighborhood issues, social activities, and worked with welfare department officials to solve individual complaints about the administration of welfare within their local area.

In 1968, a new group of more militant welfare mothers in Minneapolis came together to form Direct Action

Recipients of Welfare. Several leaders of the AFDC
League became involved in the Direct Action group
and as a result tended to become more assertive in
their dealings with local welfare administrators.
A conservative faction remained in the Minneapolis
AFDC League, however. For the next several years
this faction, along with the Ramsey County (St.
Paul) and other county AFDC League organizations
retained the traditional strategy of "talking their
problems out" with the welfare department. No legislative proposals or lobbying took place during
this period, however.

By 1970, the AFDC League had finally disintegrated
almost completely. Doris Smith, the last state
AFDC League president, attempted to pull the state
and Hennepin County League organizations back together in the spring of that year. She contacted
the few remaining active members of the AFDC League
in St. Paul, Duluth, St. Cloud, and Minneapolis and
invited them to a meeting in the Minneapolis YWCA.
There she attempted to reform the AFDC League under
a new name, the State Poor People's Coalition. Doris
openly admitted that this attempt to revitalize the
AFDC League was a result of the activities of the
Minnesota Welfare Rights Organization, which was
just beginning to organize in Minneapolis. She
indicated that many old AFDC League members had
called her to urge that the AFDC League become active again in order to counteract the militant and
less "respectable" image of welfare mothers which
was being generated by MWRO's sit-ins and demonstrations. This attempted revival failed in a few
months, however. Although several women attended
the 1970 Minnesota Welfare Association convention
meetings as representatives of the AFDC League, the
organization in the state consisted primarily of an
informal network of leaders who passed information
along to each other about what was happening in
welfare and who did minor grievance work for individuals. Only the Ramsey County AFDC League in St.
Paul, which at that point functioned solely as a
social group, sent a representative to testify at
the legislative hearings of 1970-71. The rest of
the organization had disappeared.

Welfare administrators, however, were not aware of
the collapse of the organization until the winter of

1971 when John Frederick, the new director of the Hennepin County Welfare Department, was unsuccessful in contacting the AFDC League so that a representative of the group could be appointed to the new county advisory committee.

Direct Action Recipients of Welfare

As with the AFDC League, there were a number of differing versions of how Direct Action was organized, but the following is a fairly accurate composite account.

The original idea of establishing a new group emerged in discussions among the staff and members of a local community organization called the Minneapolis Community Urban Project (MCUP), which was involved in a wide range of local issues. Early in 1968, several of the MCUP members (who also happened to be welfare recipients) had attended an NWRO Conference in Washington, D.C. One of these women stated that she came back from this meeting with a "broader perspective on where other states were with reference to the welfare battle;" others, however, were not as impressed. Nevertheless, the women agreed that it was time to take more "direct action" against the welfare department.

As news of this new group spread around the city, participants in other groups, including AFDC League members, became actively involved in Direct Action while retaining their membership and interest in their original group. Still the organization remained a small one, consisting of about 25 members during the single year of its existence.

Direct Action conducted two major campaigns during this year. The first was a "utilities campaign" to pressure the utilities company into making it easier for recipients to be put on a budget plan, thus spreading their heating payments over the whole year. The second campaign focused on obtaining a special $25 grant for school clothing for each child on welfare in Hennepin County.

According to a Direct Action member, the group's strategy was designed to "impress but not frighten"

41

welfare officials. For example, the women were prepared to follow up their small demonstrations at the welfare department with a period of lengthy negotiations in order to achieve an agreement. This evidently was a successful choice of tactics, for Direct Action won both these campaigns. A special grant was given to the children of any family requesting it for school clothing, and having gained the support of the welfare department, Direct Action successfully pressured the utilities company into making the budget plan more readily available to welfare recipients.

By the summer of 1969, Direct Action members came into increasing contact with NWRO. For example, a woman named Tina Czernek moved to Minneapolis with her husband when he was transferred there by the army. She had been on welfare previously in Massachusetts and a member of the Boston Welfare Rights Organization. Tina contacted Direct Action and agreed to work with them as a member of their staff. According to AFDC League leaders, she promised to introduce only the idea of NWRO into Minneapolis, rather than actually recruit. This informal understanding proved to be one of the sources of the later hostility between AFDC League leaders and MWRO after active welfare rights recruiting began several months later. A second contact with NWRO took place when several members of Direct Action again attended an NWRO convention. Some returned enthusiastic about the organization, but others were disillusioned. They described NWRO as "East Coast dominated and 90% black" and stated that NWRO was too concerned with building an organization at the expense of nonorganized recipients.

Those Direct Action members who were not interested in NWRO soon drifted away and became involved in starting a used clothing store and a rotating credit association for their members. Others became active again in local AFDC League groups. Those members of Direct Action who were enthusiastic about NWRO, however, became the nucleus of recruiters for a local WRO group, the Minnesota Welfare Rights Organization.

The Minnesota Welfare Rights Organization (MWRO)

Between the fall of 1969 and 1972, when the organization became dormant, MWRO was involved in five major campaigns. These five campaigns included: (1) a winter clothing campaign and (2) a furniture campaign, both of which were directed at the welfare department; (3) a Title I campaign for school clothing grants from the county school board; (4) attempts to avert reductions in the welfare budget by the state legislature and state Department of Public Welfare; and (5) demonstrations aimed at blocking the destruction of low-income housing in the city by a private apartment builder. These campaigns can be grouped into two phases and related to a similar shift which occurred in NWRO's goals. The initial phase encompassed the first two campaigns and focused on militant confrontations with the welfare system. The second phase, which began in 1970, included the last three campaigns and showed an increasing interest in nonwelfare issues and a willingness to combine conventional tactics, such as lobbying with MWRO's typical confrontation politics.

To a large extent, the strategies used by both NWRO and its local affiliate, MWRO, were influenced by events originating outside the Welfare Mothers Movement. For example, according to Minter (1970), the welfare system was particularly vulnerable when WROs first began to organize welfare mothers. Welfare agencies were under a great deal of conflicting pressure from all sides: from elected officials, from welfare recipients demanding citizen participation, and even welfare department staff pressing for "worker control." As indicated above, Piven and Cloward (1971) have suggested that much of this pressure ultimately stemmed from black unrest in the cities, from the experience of the Civil Rights Movement, and from the OEO antipoverty programs which provided welfare organizers, who worked to put increasing numbers of the poor on the welfare rolls, and poverty lawyers, who brought welfare litigation.

The initial issue around which MWRO was organized was a demand for a special clothing grant from the Hennepin County (Minneapolis) Welfare Department. This was part of a nation-wide drive on this issue initiated by NWRO. Recruiting began in the late summer of 1969. Tina Czernek contacted several philanthropic and church organizations in Minneapolis. She managed to obtain a number of grants totalling several thousand dollars to pay for her salary and to rent an office from which to organize a WRO chapter in the city. Having found a temporary office in a Minneapolis church, a massive door-knocking campaign for members was begun. Areas in the city where large numbers of welfare mothers might be expected to live were canvassed and recipients urged to join MWRO so that they could get an extra winter clothing allowance for their children.

The winter clothing campaign. The first action by MWRO occurred when a group of several hundred men, women, and children marched to the Hennepin County Welfare Department. The MWRO members submitted forms indicating what kind of winter clothing their families required, made statements explaining their demands to Eugene Heber, the director of the department, and to the assembled media, and then indicated they would return in a week to get their checks. The next week most of the requests were denied. Only those who had been on welfare for less than six months were given money to bring them up to county clothing standards under existing welfare rules. The women then began a series of sit-ins at the welfare department, and at the same time appealed the county decision to the state Department of Public Welfare. At no time did MWRO leaders give any indication that they were willing to negotiate, and the repeated requests by welfare department officials to sit down with a few of the leaders to discuss the matter were rejected on the grounds that the mothers were "sick of being represented" and wanted to participate directly in any decisions that were made. Police were called in to clear the building at closing time each day and several women were arrested and charged with disturbing the peace. (Most were later acquitted; a few were placed on one year's probation.)

In February of 1970, the state Department of Public Welfare also rejected MWRO's appeal for an extra winter clothing allotment. Thus, the clothing campaign had not been a successful one from the point of view of most MWRO members, who had hoped they

44

would receive some financial benefit from their participation. It is instructive, therefore, to compare Direct Action's campaign for a school clothing grant with the winter clothing campaign conducted by MWRO just a year later. While Direct Action was successful, MWRO met with dramatic opposition from the county welfare department and was denied the clothing money. The two campaigns differed very little, however, up to the point of the MWRO sit-ins. Thus it would seem that the public nature of MWRO's confrontations (the press was present at MWRO's request), the number of recipients involved, and the tone of the statements made (i.e., the MWRO "demands")--rather than the financial issue--were crucial factors in determining the welfare department's reaction.

The furniture campaign. Immediately after the end of the clothing campaign, a WRO group was formed in neighboring St. Paul and MWRO planned a coordinated campaign to obtain higher furniture and appliance allotments than were currently given on the basic grant. Because MWRO had been frustrated in its attempt to conduct a successful clothing campaign, the organization was looking to this new issue to bring back old members as well as new recruits. A week before the campaign was planned to begin, however, the Hennepin County Welfare Board changed the welfare regulations concerning furniture.

According to board members, the issue of furniture allotments had been under consideration for some time, but having received advance notice of the proposed MWRO campaign, at least some board members decided it might undermine MWRO's action if some changes were effected before their demonstration began. (MWRO participants charged that AFDC League members were the ones who had informed the welfare board of their upcoming campaign.) The board's changes included abolishing the inefficient and unpopular voucher system, which had required recipients to pay for furniture with a welfare department voucher rather than cash, and revising upwards the amount of money allowed for specific items of furniture--although not to the level which MWRO was to demand a week later.

MWRO leaders and staff decided to go ahead with the planned campaign on the grounds that the new allotments

were still not high enough to allow welfare mothers
to buy new furniture and appliances. The women objected to buying second-hand appliances particularly because they were usually over-priced and needed
more frequent repair than new items. MWRO members
turned in their request forms for furniture at a
meeting of the Hennepin County Welfare Board and
promised to return for a decision at next week's
regularly scheduled meeting.

Television crews were present to film this board
meeting the following week. The welfare board chair,
Dick Peterson, allowed the approximately 50-60 MWRO
members to state their case, and then called upon
anyone else in the audience to speak if they wished
to rebut MWRO's statements. Spokesmen from a group
which called itself Wonderful Opportunities, Rewards
Keen (WORK) stood up to oppose MWRO's demands for a
further increase in the furniture allotments. The
thrust of the WORK members' comments was that all
recipients were lazy, gambling, promiscuous women
who did not deserve the money that was spent on them
in the first place. After WORK members had voiced
their opposition, the welfare board called for a
vote, and unanimously rejected MWRO's demands and
immediately adjourned the meeting. Individual
members of WORK and MWRO engaged in heated arguments
for several minutes until MWRO's organizer, Tina
Czernek, loudly announced she was going next door to
the welfare department and demand to see the director.
Most of the women followed her.

A sit-in resulted from this action. The welfare
department director, Eugene Heber, hinted that the
women would again meet with arrest if they stayed
past closing time, and refused to bargain with MWRO
on the grounds that he was bound by the decision of
the welfare board. The mothers sat in the lobby of
the building for several hours, but all agreed quietly
that the group was to leave at closing time, as no
one was prepared to be arrested again. Carl Jones,
a minister who supported MWRO, suggested to Tina
that he return to meet with the chair of the welfare
board and set up negotiations. Tina agreed. Soon
meetings between Peterson and several MWRO leaders
and staff were arranged which resulted in the establishment of friendly relations.

In spite of the series of meetings which took place
between Peterson and the women, however, the welfare
board did not reverse its decision to maintain the
furniture allotments at the current revised level.
Peterson later told me that as a result of their
visits with him, however, he felt that MWRO leaders
had become more moderate; they were "willing to
communicate, to wade through emotions, and get down
to action in solving their problems." At the same
time, he admitted that the meetings had changed his
attitudes as well. He was now "inclined to accept
things that MWRO does--based on the leadership I know."

Many MWRO participants also felt that something had
been gained from the campaign. Carl Jones pointed
out, for instance, that as a result of the clothing
and furniture campaigns:

> Welfare Rights had gained legitimacy by speak-
> ing out, being visible, so that whereas before
> people thought the welfare department spoke for
> welfare recipients, most think Welfare Rights
> does now and will ask for them. WRO has become
> institutionalized as something welfare recip-
> ients belong to.

In spite of this visibility, however, after the furniture campaign ended the organization gradually lost
its active membership. The local VISTA staff also
began to get involved in other groups, and by the
summer of 1970--a year after she came to Minneapolis--
Tina Czernek left the city with her husband.

The leaders of several neighborhood locals in
Minneapolis began meeting as a single group at this
time, with Carl Jones contributing a great deal of
time and moral support to keep the group functioning.
For example, he encouraged the women to plan a small
campaign, and they decided upon a "birthday party"
for NWRO. Gifts such as a dead mouse and a sock
with a hole in it were presented before the assembled
media to welfare department officials. In addition,
the few remaining active MWRO members attended an
NWRO conference and established personal relationships
with several NWRO leaders and staff. All these activities helped develop a feeling of camaraderie among
the mothers. As Carl Jones told me:

47

> There's one thing that has helped cement the
> group together and that was going through--
> well, they've had a history. Any group that
> has a history, a tradition--that tradition
> tends to hold them together. And there was a
> bit of suffering in that tradition and a bit
> of glory in the sense of a sit-in demonstration
> and in the sense of being arrested together,
> in jail together, and going to court together.

In the fall of 1970, a husband and wife WRO organizing team, the Bernsteins, were hired by MWRO to take
over Tina Czernek's old position. Their hiring
marked the beginning of the second phase of MWRO
activity which involved a new interest in pursuing
nonwelfare issues. The new strategy included public
confrontations, as in the past, but there was a
willingness on the part of MWRO to enter into negotiations more readily than before. Whenever possible,
MWRO leaders and staff tried to avoid an open show-
down--although publicly their statements remained
militant and intransigent.

Several internal and external factors were instrumental in bringing about this change in strategy.
First, several of MWRO's leaders had been placed on
probation as a result of the sit-ins at the welfare
department, and so could not afford to be arrested
again. They were reluctant to ask other members to
engage in sit-ins, therefore, if they as leaders
would not be at risk as well.

Second, the organizers were very influential in determining the tactics for MWRO campaigns. The
Bernsteins told me that they believed that Tina had
made some tactical mistakes while she was organizer
in the state. For example, Tina had been involved
with WRO in Boston where the welfare department was
decentralized, with isolated neighborhood offices
which could easily be overwhelmed by relatively small
groups of WRO participants. In Minneapolis, however,
the welfare department was housed in a centrally
located multistory downtown building which could not
easily be shut down by an MWRO sit-in.

Third, NWRO was trying to broaden the appeal of the
organization at this time by extending membership

eligibility to members of the working poor and planning campaigns on issues which would be of interest to this group as well as to welfare mothers. In addition, NWRO strategists were deeply involved in planning and implementing a lobbying campaign designed to defeat Nixon's proposed Family Assistance Plan.

Fourth, events in the larger society also had an effect on the strategy MWRO used. The local political climate had grown less tolerant of recipient protests due to concern over rising taxes in the state. The legislature was facing a budgetary crisis and many legislators were prepared to cut welfare appropriations. Even Minneapolis had moved from a period of liberal city government into a taxpayer/silent majority backlash that culminated in the election of a conservative former police detective as mayor of the city. Changes were also taking place in the Hennepin County Welfare Department. A new director, John Frederick, was hired and although he was not especially supportive of MWRO's goals, he did show some interest in meeting with the organization on a regular basis. Nationally the climate had also shifted due in large part to what NWRO perceived as President Nixon's conservative social philosophy and a general turn toward the right by many Americans.

Three major campaigns were undertaken by MWRO between 1970 and 1972 during this second phase. Only two of these campaigns were actually initiated by MWRO, however. The third was a reaction by MWRO and a number of other organizations in the state to a series of measures designed to reduce welfare spending.

The Title I campaign. Immediately after they came to Minnesota, the Bernsteins urged that MWRO conduct a Title I campaign. Title I was that portion of the Elementary and Secondary Education Act which allocated federal money to school districts for each child who performed below the national norms in subjects such as reading and mathematics. The money was to be used for teacher's aides, as well as for a variety of other measures designed to bring the children up to the national average. According to NWRO's research on Title I law, local WROs had a good chance of success on this issue. Accordingly, MWRO demanded: (1) that the county school board use some of the

49

Title I funds for winter school clothing so poor
children could attend class, and thus improve their
performance in school; and (2) that the board immediately establish a parents advisory board (in accordance with federal law) which was to be consulted on
how Title I funds were to be spent.

The tactics used in this campaign were essentially
similar to those of the previous year. About 200
women and children were bussed to the school administration building to hand in request forms and speak
at a meeting of the Board of Education. The board,
however, refused to use what it called "education
money" for clothing.[1] When MWRO leaders returned to
another school board meeting to continue to press
their demands, one board member announced that he
had discussed MWRO's demands with the Urban Coalition
(of which he was also a member) and that it had a-
greed to give MWRO $10,000 to be distributed through
school social workers to all families which requested
it. As a result, MWRO leaders felt that they had
salvaged a victory out of the campaign. Furthermore,
the Title I campaign had succeeded in getting some
of the working poor to join MWRO.

Threatened welfare reductions. Before MWRO had an
opportunity to plan a new campaign, events in the
larger society overtook them in the form of a number
of proposals which were designed to cut welfare expenditures. The Bernsteins urged the welfare mothers
to adopt what they called a "middle-class" approach
to dealing with these financial crises, rather than
the usual pattern of confrontation. Both the welfare
mothers and staff initially were very pessimistic,
however, about the chance of averting these proposed
cutbacks.

The first proposal came from the state Department of
Public Welfare. In response to an HEW ruling that
uniform grant levels had to be established within a
state in order for that state to continue receiving
matching federal monies, the state welfare system
developed a "flat grant" system. Required to hold
a public hearing on this proposal, the state welfare
system was unprepared for the negative reactions it
got from recipient organizations, such as the AFDC
League and MWRO, from urban welfare departments (who

50

opposed lowering their grants to the proposed uniform level), and from rural departments (who did not want to have to spend as much as the flat grant would have required). In the face of this extensive opposition, the state Commissioner of Welfare abandoned the proposed plan, but warned that the legislature might make even more drastic reductions on its own.

At this public hearing, MWRO relied on legal arguments and an orderly presentation of the negative impact such a flat grant system would have on the lives of most welfare recipients. For example, as the hearing began, Sam Putnam, MWRO's lawyer, pointed out that less than the required thirty days notice had been given by the department. Putnam explained that MWRO was attending under protest, therefore, and indicated the group might contest the results of the hearing (if, indeed the flat grant system was instituted) on the grounds of this legal technicality. At Leslie Bernstein's suggestion, MWRO spokeswomen tried to avoid a "free-for-all with people yelling out of the crowd." In spite of this, the hearing was not completely free of disruption. For example, halfway through MWRO's presentation the Commissioner interrupted and asked for someone with an opposing view to speak, but MWRO refused to yield the microphone, shouting down the Commissioner's objections.

Soon after the flat grant hearing, some members of the state legislature did propose a 10% cut in welfare appropriations. MWRO staff members were contacted by the director of the Hennepin County Welfare Department, who suggested that the two groups could work together to avert the cutback. Toward this end, the welfare department supplied MWRO with some of the statistics needed for their presentations and sent a representative of the county to the state legislature to lobby against the proposal. A state senator who opposed the reduction in welfare spending also approached the MWRO organizers--offering his help in planning the group's strategy and coaching the welfare mothers on the types of facts the legislators would demand from their testimony and on the proper rules of behavior. Individual MWRO members began to buttonhole legislators, testified at legis-

lative sessions and public hearings, and encouraged
MWRO supporters to send letters and telegrams ex-
pressing opposition to any reduction in welfare funding. For the first time, MWRO began to actively
look for support from a wide variety of nonwelfare
organizations in the state, including social work
groups, liberal church groups, ethnic organizations,
and other "human rights" movements.

When the Minnesota State Legislature eventually
voted to retain welfare appropriations at the current levels, MWRO members and staff felt that their
lobbying efforts had played a major part in averting
the cutback. The women also emphasized the positive
impact that MWRO's "myth sheet" had had. This was
a flier sent to all legislators which was designed
to dispel many of the misconceptions the average
person has about welfare recipients. The sheet
compared the amount of welfare fraud with the amount
of Internal Revenue Service fraud, presented figures
on the average length of time on welfare and the
actual amount of illegitimacy among welfare mothers,
and pointed out that most recipients were unable
to work for valid reasons (they were children, elder-
ly, or disabled).

A final attempt to reduce the amount of money being
spent on welfare in the state involved a proposal
by the state Department of Public Welfare to establish a "shelter maxima" plan. Like the earlier
flat grant plan, the state welfare system justified
this proposal on the grounds that it was designed
to bring the state into compliance with the federal
directive that there be uniform grant levels in the
state. This new plan attempted to incorporate many
of the objections voiced about the flat grant system
by establishing two state-wide uniform maximum
grants for housing--one level for urban counties
and a lower level for rural ones. The maximum grant
for housing in urban counties was still below the
actual cost of housing in most cities in Minnesota,
however, especially Minneapolis.

MWRO organizers were informed in advance of this
shelter maxima proposal by a social worker sympathetic
to the group who worked in the Hennepin County Welfare
Department. MWRO's lawyer, Sam Putnam, then began a

series of discussions with Frederick, the county director. They informally agreed that Putnam should request an injunction on the state Department of Public Welfare so that the plan could not be implemented immediately, thus giving the county time to pressure the state to devise a more liberal plan. According to Putnam, the director had urged him to take this action against the state since the county welfare department, as part of the welfare system, could not. This tactic was successful in postponing a decision on the exact plan to be developed by the state to achieve uniform grant levels. A flat grant system was instituted, however, the following year. By that time MWRO was no longer a functioning organization.

The housing campaign. MWRO's final campaign was planned as an indirect means of pressuring the state Department of Public Welfare to liberalize the housing grants in the proposed shelter maxima plan (whose implementation MWRO was legally delaying at the time). This last campaign began in June of 1971 and was directed at a large private building contractor in Minneapolis. Carl Jones had learned that this contractor had been investigated by the Minneapolis Tenants Union, which believed that it was vulnerable to public pressure about its business practices. This company was one of the most active in building a large number of middle-income rental units in deteriorating Model Cities areas, thus aggravating the low-income housing crisis the city already faced.

The strategy agreed on by MWRO leaders and members of the Tenants Union marked a return to MWRO's typical pattern of confrontation and demonstrations. MWRO leaders insisted that the first step in the campaign be a series of demonstrations to publicize their complaints and, hopefully, to create public support for their proposals (to rent 20% of the vacant apartments to the poor at current Hennepin County Welfare Department housing allowances). Only if this tactic failed to work would the two organizations proceed with the Tenants Union's suggestion that they occupy one of the corporation's buildings.

After a week of demonstrations at the corporation

53

offices, the president set up a negotiating session with MWRO representatives at a nearby church. Over the objections of the corporation and three supporters it had brought from the Minneapolis Apartment Association and Housing Institute, the media were allowed to film the discussion which took place before a large audience of MWRO participants, members of WORK, and the general public. The corporation first argued that it would lose money by renting the apartments at a low price (although they frequently advertised special rent reduction offers in the newspapers). They also tried to divert attention to a discussion of "industry-wide problems" as a whole. Finally, they asked MWRO to support the corporation's own request to the federal government for a subsidy so that rents could be lowered to a level low-income people could afford. MWRO spokeswomen firmly rejected these proposals and insisted on an immediate reply to their own demands. The president of the corporation flatly rejected their proposals also.

A week later, the president's home was picketed by about 20 MWRO members and supporters. Later, in an interview, MWRO's lawyer described the picketing as a very successful action. The corporation president had evidently called an MWRO leader and told her that he was furious that his family had been humiliated before the neighbors, and demanded that MWRO not picket his home again. In spite of the lawyer's positive evaluation of the effectiveness of MWRO's action, most of the welfare mothers voted to stop picketing his home, because they could "sympathize with how he felt." Instead, small groups picketed some of the corporation's construction sites. This approach was ineffective, however, and did not generate publicity or put pressure on the corporation to reopen negotiations. No apartment building was occupied, and MWRO leaders eventually let the issue drop. As one MWRO leader later said, "The welfare department may be afraid of us, but the corporation ain't because he's private enterprise and is backed up by the Association [of Apartment Builders]."

By the fall of 1971, MWRO had ceased functioning as a group. In part this was due to the loss of their organizers, as the Bernsteins left Minneapolis to

take a job in another city. Some of the strongest
leaders in the Minneapolis and St. Paul organizations
no longer were willing to devote time to the organization or had found part-time jobs. The political
climate in the state (and the nation) remained cool
to continued protests by the welfare mothers, and
the state welfare system and legislature continued
to seek ways to reduce welfare spending. Some individuals still remained actively interested in welfare issues in Minneapolis through 1972, however.
For example, some MWRO members joined in a successful suit initiated by the Legal Aid Society to force
the welfare department to better publicize the availability of food stamps. In addition, many women
continued individual grievance work at the welfare
department and kept on giving "speaking engagements"
describing MWRO's goals to community organizations
when they were requested.

The Minnesota Recipients Alliance

In the fall of 1972 after my fieldwork was completed,
a new and again purely local group, the Minnesota
Recipients Alliance (MRA) was organized by one of
the leaders from the now defunct MWRO groups. Some
of the membership came from MWRO, but the bulk were
reported to be previously unorganized welfare recipients in Minneapolis. While I did not directly observe this group, informants stated that it remained
active for over three years. MRA ignored national
issues and focused on (1) individual grievance work
at the local welfare department; (2) small protests
and sit-ins over specific local welfare issues,
especially attempts to cut back on welfare funding;
and (3) lobbying at the 1974-75 biennial session
of the state legislature for reinstatement of certain
special grants which had been dropped from the welfare program when the flat grant system had been
implemented. They also sponsored workshops on issues
relevant to the poor, such as one to teach working
welfare recipients how to fill out income tax forms
and ways in which to keep as much of their refund
as possible from being taken by the welfare department.

MRA became involved in the same kind of issues and
supported the beliefs of the earlier MWRO groups, but

actively avoided any connection with NWRO. Their
strategy was composed of a mixture of the militant
tactics of MWRO and the more conservative approach
of the AFDC League. For example, the group staged
a sit-in at the governor's office, yet made no use
of the Legal Aid lawyers who had worked with MWRO.
In fact, there was a general consensus among movement participants that as much had been achieved on
the legal front as was feasible at that point in
time. The MRA emphasized lobbying, as had the AFDC
League, but scrupulously avoided "cooperative"
lobbying with the welfare department in order to
establish their credibility as a separate organization responsive only to the needs of welfare mothers.

National Welfare Rights Organization (NWRO)

In order to avoid interrupting the narrative of the
local history of the Welfare Mothers Movement in
Minnesota, I have left a brief history of NWRO until this point (cf. Piven and Cloward, 1971; 1977
for a more complete account of NWRO's development).
Chronologically, however, NWRO was founded only two
years after the appearance of the AFDC League in
Minnesota.

In 1966, the Poverty/Rights Action Center was established inWashington, D.C. by Dr. George A. Wiley, a
former college professor and civil rights activist.
Piven and Cloward (1977:276-8) have suggested that
Wiley formed this group in response to their ideas
as they were outlined in a mimeographed paper entitled "A Strategy to End Poverty," which they cir-
culated among organizers and civil rights leaders
in late 1965.[2] This group hoped that welfare might
prove to be a new issue around which to organize in
northern ghettos. The fact that a few welfare groups
had already formed suggested the possibility that
organizations across the country could be drawn
together into a national organization which could put
pressure on the system and bring about substantial
change in the conditions of the people living in
urban ghettos. This national organization was to
be NWRO.

On June 30, 1967 the first NWRO demonstrations were

held across the country involving approximately 5000 recipients in 44 cities and 21 states. These WROs were theoretically independent organizations linked through state representatives to a National Coordinating Committee. A newsletter, NOW! (later, the Welfare Fighter) was published in order to encourage solidarity among these scattered local groups, to publicize group successes, and otherwise maintain communication across the country. NWRO's coordinating activities were financed from membership dues, private gifts, foundation grants, and eventually HEW itself, which gave NWRO a grant to conduct a study on one of its own welfare programs. In addition, the Friends of Welfare Rights was established as a category from which financial and other types of support could be channeled into local WROs (Steiner, 1971:283-9).

Piven and Cloward (1977:28-5) report that they urged NWRO to adopt a strategy of mobilizing welfare recipients for disruptive activities. While this advice ran counter to much conventional political wisdom and standard organizing doctrines, Piven and Cloward based this new strategy on their analysis of successful social movements among the poor: the political system seemed to be unresponsive to poor people's organizations but responded quickly to disruptive protests, particularly in Northern industrial states crucial to the fortunes of the Democratic Party.

Wiley and other NWRO organizers viewed this strategy as overly manipulative, rather than democratic, and as risky for recipients, who might be exposed to retaliation by local elites. Instead NWRO formulated a two-pronged strategy. The initial tactics were militant confrontations with the welfare system designed to get all those eligible on the welfare rolls, thus "bankrupting" the system and forcing its reform. At the same time, NWRO organizers were to work to build stable organizations around the country which could advance their interests in much the same way as labor unions did for workers. NWRO strategists felt they could thus not only obtain increased welfare benefits and economic aid for the poor, but also work for the long-term goal of a national income standard (Steiner, 1971).

Under the slogan, "Guaranteed Income, Dignity, Justice

and Democracy," WROs mounted large-scale campaigns
to obtain benefits and concentrated on gaining
access to local welfare Manuals in order to spread
information about welfare entitlements to recipients,
and in order to do effective grievance work for WRO
members. According to Steiner (1971:282-3), the
tactics WROs used were basically nonviolent, militant (though usually legal) confrontations involving weeks of demonstrations at local welfare offices,
and on one occasion at HEW, in order to harass or
disrupt business.

In the summer of 1969, however, NWRO strategists decided to broaden the base of the organization beyond its original AFDC constituency. NWRO was to
become a multi-constituency, multi-issue organization (Piven & Cloward, 1967:312). Increased political strength was to be achieved by extending membership eligibility to all people with incomes below
NWRO's adequate income standard (which was then
$5500 for a four-person family) and by working on
nonwelfare issues, such as health care, problems of
the aged, etc. Piven and Cloward (1977:316) contend
that by 1970 it was clear that NWRO was in great
difficulty, despite these attempts to expand membership:

> NWRO's organizational apparatus expanded in
> the period between 1969 and 1972. The national
> budget rose, the national staff grew, and
> NWRO's national reputation enlarged. That this
> could be so was a consequence of a swelling
> tide of public support from outside sources. . .
> churchmen, public officials, social welfare
> organizations, unions, civil rights groups,
> foundations, media representatives. But this
> enlarging flow of resources undermined organi-
> zing. NWRO was transformed from a protest organ-
> ization to a negotiating and lobbying organization.

NWRO's major lobbying effort focused on the defeat
of Nixon's welfare reform package, the Family Assistance Plan, which was introduced into the Congress
in 1970. Eventually defeated in 1972, there is some
debate over the effectiveness of NWRO's lobbying efforts; Piven and Cloward (1977:342-5) point out that
NWRO claimed a great deal of credit for the defeat of

the bill. They suggest, however, that more important were Nixon's withdrawal of support from his own bill and opposition to the reform plan both from fiscal conservatives, who felt the bill was too generous, and from liberals, who along with NWRO disliked the forced work provisions and low guaranteed annual income level. This new use of conventional political tactics by NWRO reached its peak during 1972 when NWRO members were urged to become delegates to the National Democratic Convention. WRO strategists hoped to pressure the party to follow its new rules on delegate selection which allocated a certain number of delegates to representatives of selected categories, such as the poor. Not only would NWRO members be "politicized" through their participation in party politics, but it was hoped that organized welfare recipients could become a part of the traditional coalition of groups composing the Democratic Party.

The organization increasingly lost momentum, however, between 1972 and 1974 when NWRO declared bankruptcy and closed its Washington, D.C. office. A number of factors appear to be involved. First, many members believed they had achieved no significant impact on the policies of the Democratic Party--which itself suffered a defeat with the re-election of Richard Nixon. Many local WROs began complaining that NWRO had expended too many of the organization's resources on national issues and neglected local campaigns more relevant to members' immediate concerns (Piven & Cloward, 1971:349-52). Second, with the defeat of FAP, welfare reform as an issue lost its appeal, and the focus of national attention soon turned to the problem of political corruption symbolized by Watergate. Third, WROs all over the country lost experienced organizers and leaders who became involved in other organizations or movements, found employment, or became interested in city or county government (Hertz, 1978).

The history of the Welfare Mothers Movement clearly shows a pattern of the disappearance of established groups and the continual emergence of new groups within the movement over the years. These fluctuations were largely adaptive responses to changes in the political climate and in the availability of resources to support Welfare Mothers Movement activity.

From this perspective, the appearance of Welfare

Mothers Movement groups in the mid-1960s was an important event in its own right. Traditionally there have been more limitations placed on the political activities of welfare mothers than on those of the average citizen. Until the 1960s there were only two alternatives open to recipients: (1) take no political or other action to redress legal-administrative grievances; or (2) take individual action. A third alternative did not emerge for AFDC mothers until new moral, legal and governmental resources were introduced into the arena through the Great Society programs of the 1960s. This third alternative was for welfare mothers to organize and work as a group to solve problems in the welfare system and to overcome their political powerlessness.

FOOTNOTES

1. Ironically, it was reported over a year later in the Ithaca _Journal_ (February 11, 1972) that Minnesota was among those states accused of misspending millions of dollars of Title I funds over a number of years. The funds involved were those spent by the school boards to build a library and to supplement teacher salaries. Repayment of one-half these funds to HEW was required of the state.

2. This article was later printed as "A Strategy to End Poverty" in _The Nation_ 202:510-17 on May 2, 1966.

CHAPTER 4

Organization

When Americans think of "organization," we usually
think of a "pyramidal bureaucratic structure with
some central authority, hierarchical leadership,
and a clear channel of command" (Gerlach & Hine,
1973:163-4). If there is no obvious structure of
this type, we tend to assume either that people are
unorganized and acting only as a collection of unrelated and fragmented groups, or that a small covert elite is actually controlling them. Gerlach
and Hine suggest, however, that there is a third
kind of structure characteristic of social movements
to which we are not culturally accustomed (and which
may be disconcerting to movement participants as
well, if they decide that their movement should have
the kind of stable, centralized structure characteristic of establishment organizations). This third
kind of organization is adaptive in promoting change,
however, just as bureaucratic structures are effective in routinized activities which serve to maintain social stability. Social movements, then, are
characterized by a segmentary, decentralized, and
reticulate organization (Gerlach & Hine, 1970:34-56).[1]

By segmentary, Gerlach and Hine mean that a typical
movement is made up of semiautonomous segments or
cells which are formed in a variety of ways. Since
there is no single leader who can make binding
decisions for all movement participants about goals,
tactics, or ideology, groups may proliferate whenever members wish to break off from a parent organization and attack their problems in a different way.
Personality clashes between leaders and other petty
differences may be the source of segmentation, as
well as pre-existing social, cultural, or geographical cleavages. In addition, there are always some
cells in the organization of a movement which develop
quite independently of any other group in response
to new local or national conditions.

According to Gerlach and Hine (1973:165), these semiautonomous groups:

    Vary in size, internal organization, ideological

stance, and kinds of methods they deem appropriate for the achievement of movement goals. Some are small local groups operating without benefit of by-laws, formal officers, or membership requirements other than presence at meetings. Others are more formally structured with membership dues, designated leaders, and regional and national offices. Newspaper reports of movement activities frequently focus on such recognizable segments. But the structural strength of any movement rests as much upon the activities of the hundreds of small groups which operate independently of, and frequently in opposition to, the larger cells.

A second characteristic of movement organization is its decentralization. No single leader or efficient coordinating body speaks for or controls all movement groups. Each group has its own leader(s) who occasionally have influence outside their own organization as long as they continue to fulfill their role successfully and prove their value to movement groups. The leader may be the extremely charismatic individual with a large personal following who was focused on in the early work on social movements (e.g., Wallace, 1956), but more frequently the leader is simply no more than one among many members who may have some charismatic ability to influence others. Loss of support, removal by the opposition, or selling out to the establishment simply leads to his or her quick replacement by another leader.

Third, movement organization is reticulate. Groups within the movement frequently divide to form smaller units, but also combine to form larger configurations in certain circumstances. Groups within the movement are linked into a network in a variety of ways: (1) by means of overlapping membership of individual participants; (2) through intersecting relationships between group leaders of different cells; (3) through the actions of traveling evangelists or speakers who move through the movement network effecting communication, contributing to movement cohesion, or achieving a measure of ideological unity; and (4) through certain "ritual" activities, such as conferences, mass rallies, or national demonstrations. These national coalitions or large-scale actions are a means for different segments of the movement to temporarily come together for a single purpose, to exchange ideas, and to focus public attention on movement goals.

Such demonstrations are frequently viewed by outsiders as the very purpose of the movement and their success, therefore, is seen as a measure of its strength. Small groups which do not regularly appear at hearings or demonstrations are dismissed as ineffective or may not even be considered part of the movement. Such a view misses the whole point. A movement is not just a collection of protest activities, but a social organization characterized by a segmented, decentralized and reticulate structure (Gerlach & Hine, 1973:166). Observers, however, often underestimate the effectiveness of movement organization by ignoring the role of these small, local, ad hoc groups, or condemn this form of organization as defective, divisive, or wasteful of participants' limited energies.

The idea that organization is "at best a diversion and frequently counterproductive" is, however, the main thesis of Piven and Cloward's (1977) work on poor people's movements in the United States (Jenkins, 1979:222-3). They argue that the limited gains that movements of the poor historically have achieved in this country have come entirely from mass insurgency (strikes, riots, marches), and not from organizing participants into stable, enduring groups. Activists have usually concentrated on developing formally structured bureaucratic organizations, however, because they believed this was necessary in order for public or private elites to be forced into making the concessions or changes demanded by the movement (and which are necessary for the movement's continued growth and expansion). Piven and Cloward suggest that elites do seek out existing organizations of the poor, but not because they have been influenced by the activities of those groups. Rather the elites are responding to the underlying force of insurgency which has briefly emerged among some segment of the population. The only lower-class organizations which tend to survive, then, are those which abandon their oppositional politics and draw people away from the streets and into the meetings rooms, thus facilitating the efforts

of the elites to channel insurgent masses into conventional politics. Movement organizations are,
therefore, extremely vulnerable to cooptation according to their analysis. A group which has come to
depend upon any kind of elites--from the press to
public officials--for financial support, the confer-
ral of legitimacy and recognition, or political
status (or even the appearance of possessing conventional political influence) is unlikely to cause
further disturbance (Piven & Cloward, 1977:320-4).

As a result of this analysis, Piven and Cloward
(1977:283-5) argued that, instead of welfare organizations, a loose-knit cadre of students, organizers,
civil rights activists and militant AFDC recipients
should have been formed to heighten the crisis
caused by the Civil Rights Movement and rioting in
the cities. This "organization of organizers"
would not build local organizations to obtain local
victories, but would try to create a series of disruptions and a rise in the welfare rolls to which
the federal government would have to respond.
According to Piven and Cloward, however, NWRO leaders and staff did not choose to go along with their
strategy of mobilizing rather than organizing.
These leaders believed that the poor could be influential if brought together into a national organization. NWRO leaders also feared that a mobilizing
strategy, as distinct from an organizing strategy,
would give the poor little control over the direction of the movement and the local crises it might
generate, and that such tactics were a manipulative
rather than democratic approach to the poor. Instead,
NWRO strategists turned their energy toward developing a nationally coordinated organization in which
policies and strategies were to be determined by
the poor, with the role of staff members subordinated
to that of the recipient leaders. The staff were to
offer technical assistance, such as researching complex welfare regulations, while developing training
programs to teach political and leadership skills to
WRO members with the expectation that the role of
organizer would eventually wither away.

An analysis of both the organization and actual internal political processes found in Welfare Mothers
Movement groups in Minnesota will provide some inde-

pendent material with which to judge Piven and
Cloward's hypotheses about movement organization
and their description of the respective activities
of the staff and recipient leaders in the WRO segment of the movement. In the process, two related
points will be made. First, as Jenkins (1979:226)
contends, Piven and Cloward's thesis clearly pre-
sents too simple a picture of the organizational
options (militant cadre vs. quiescent bureaucracy)
available to social movements. Second, Piven and
Cloward, by narrowly focusing on a single organiza-
tion--NWRO, have misunderstood the real extent of
movement activity in time and space, and have under-
estimated the adaptive qualities of the actual form
of organization found to be characteristic of the
Welfare Mothers Movement.

The Expansion of the AFDC League

Initially the AFDC League was composed of a single
group of about eighty women. The organization focused
on establishing itself as a viable, visible group and
on influencing passage of amendments to the state
welfare laws during the 1965 biennial legislative
session. Offices were kept to a minimum and most
business was conducted through ad hoc committees or
by a few informal leaders in a "behind the scenes"
fashion, as they put it. By the summer of 1965,
however, about a half-dozen new groups had formed
around the state--primarily in urban rather than
rural counties. At the same time, the organization
in the Twin Cities split into two groups along county
lines (Ramsey County/St. Paul and Hennepin County/
Minneapolis). These organizations further split into
neighborhood-level "satellite groups."

County and satellite groups proliferated in three
ways: (1) small, local pre-existing groups of welfare recipients would hear about the AFDC League's
activities and ask to affiliate with it, or the smaller group would gradually lose its membership to the
AFDC League as a result of overlapping participation;
(2) members of an established AFDC League group would
split off and form a separate group based on a smaller
geographic area or on the basis of race;[2] or (3) the
professional staff of a neighborhood settlement house

65

or private social workers in other cities would
hear about the AFDC League and ask that a speaker
be sent to their group. This often led to the formation of a new AFDC League chapter or the affiliation of an existing group with the organization.

A state level of organization was formed in 1966
through the establishment of a State AFDC League
Board composed of one delegate and one alternate
from each county organization. Groups at each level
(state, county, and neighborhood) had their own
officers (a president, vice-president, secretary,
and treasurer), and if they could find one, a volunteer staff person who was willing to work with the
organization. Both the neighborhood and county
AFDC League groups could plan independent activities,
but were also expected to send representatives to
participate in statewide efforts. In actual practice,
however, the state-level organization of the AFDC
League consisted largely of the two county groups in
the Twin Cities. State meetings were usually held
in the Twin Cities, not only because these groups
had the largest membership, but also because June
Waldheim, the YWCA Activities Coordinator who worked
with the AFDC League, was based in Minneapolis.
Since the major function of the State AFDC League
Board was to plan the organization's lobbying efforts,
it was generally agreed that the state president also
should live near enough to St. Paul, the state
capitol, to keep on top of political events both
during and after the biennial legislative sessions.

Most of the county AFDC League organizations outside
the Twin Cities remained small and engaged primarily
in social activities or local grievance work throughout the year. It was difficult for the members of
these county groups to participate continuously in
the state-level organization because they lacked the
money for travel or even frequent telephone calls to
the Twin Cities area, and the women had difficulty
in finding someone to care for their children if
they left town for AFDC League functions. In order
to overcome this problem in communication, a newsletter, the Cradle Rocker Crier, was begun as a
means of linking local and county groups together by
reporting the activities and successes of AFDC League
organizations around the state.

66

In spite of these problems, these smaller county AFDC League groups served as a pool of welfare mothers who could be called on for major political actions planned by the State AFDC League Board. At least one representative of each county group was sent to lobby or testify before the welfare sub-committees during legislative sessions. The segmentary and decentralized nature of AFDC League organization also allowed each group to contribute to the organization's goals in its own way. For example, welfare regulations and problems differed from county to county within the state (e.g., Minneapolis had high grant levels, but St. Cloud did not). The loose AFDC League organization enabled county groups to work on these local problems without cumbersome central bureaucratic direction or interference--thus putting a premium on innovation, initiative, and sensitivity to local political conditions. Such a structure also enabled the AFDC League to reach different types of women with a variety of interests and yet contain them all within a larger organization. Even if some local groups were primarily interested in social or self-help activities, all were willing to help lobby at the legislature when they were needed.

At the end of the 1967-1968 legislative session, however, the state-level AFDC League organization began to disintegrate and coordination of satellite groups within the larger cities, such as Minneapolis, became more sporadic. In typical movement style, there had always been a tendency for coordination to fall off at the end of each legislative session once opposition (in the form of conflict with the legis-lators) was withdrawn. For the first time, however, the state and county-level organization did not emerge again in late 1969 when planning for another year of lobbying should have begun. A brief attempt to pull a statewide group together again under the name, the State Poor People's Coalition, also failed.

Outsiders may have pessimistically interpreted the failure of the AFDC League to reconstruct itself as an indication that welfare mothers were unable to sustain interest in welfare reform. This conclusion would not take into account, however, the continual creation of new groups within the movement. For example, a new set of more militant welfare mothers were forming Direct Action Recipients of Welfare at this time, and many of the more active AFDC League members joined this organization as well. At the same time, a few satellite groups in Minneapolis and St. Paul continued doing individual grievance work, planning social events, and giving speeches about the AFDC League. These small-scale activities cannot be dismissed as irrelevant to the movement's goals, for they continued to bring changes into the lives of the welfare mothers who were involved in them.

The Growth of MWRO

According to the policy of NWRO, the organization was to be composed of a nationwide, statewide, and sometimes citywide system of structures. The state organizations were to be coordinated through a state Executive Committee, which was to meet at least every other month and was to be made up of state officers selected by a state convention attended by all existing "locals" within the state. The locals were the basic building block of the organization. To be legally affiliated with NWRO, locals had to consist of at least 25 members who had paid yearly dues to the national organization. They were to be organized on fairly restricted geographical areas within the state, such as the neighborhood of a city, and were to have their own by-laws and officers and were to hold monthly meetings. Each local could theoretically determine its own goals within the broad ideological framework of NWRO, although in practice MWRO locals were dependent on the national organization for planning campaigns. Whenever possible, the locals in large cities were to be coordinated through an additional citywide body of some sort, such as an Executive Committee.

On paper, this organization does indeed look like the centralized, bureaucratic organization which Piven and Cloward suggested was characteristic of NWRO. In Minnesota, however, MWRO never achieved this formal structure. Instead, for most of the group's existence, coordination occurred primarily through informal contacts between the organizers or

staff and the leaders of each local. Only for short
periods of time were the neighborhood locals linked
through monthly (or even less frequent) joint meetings. The Minneapolis and St. Paul groups maintained
contact in similar ways, although on an even more
attenuated basis, as can be seen through the following description of the organizational development
of MWRO.

The rudiments of a working organization were established at the first meeting of MWRO in the fall of
1969. At that time, a Steering Committee was elected, although this set of temporary officers was to
be replaced by an Executive Board, National Coordinating Committee representative and a Grievance Committee "as soon as everyone in the group knew each
other better," as one staff member told me. This
election took place several weeks later, about halfway through the first clothing campaign. Meetings
of the Executive Committees (which were made up of
the officers of each local and the members of their
Grievance Committees) were infrequent, however, and
tended to occur primarily just before a new campaign
was to begin. Most active leaders and staff members
reported that real decisions were made either at
staff meetings (which included only Tina Czernek,
the MWRO organizer, and the rest of the staff of
students and VISTAs), or were made over the telephone
during conversations between the staff and leaders
of each local.

By the end of the winter clothing campaign, three
more MWRO groups had been organized in Minneapolis,
bringing the total number to five. Several locals
were also formed in St. Paul, but at no time were
officers or a formal state organization set up to
coordinate the activities of the WRO groups in the
two cities. As a result, such coordination fell to
the staff, who planned a campaign for increased furniture and appliance allotments which was to be conducted simultaneously in Minneapolis and St. Paul.
An important point to note here is that a more formal,
centralized and bureaucratically structured WRO
organization could have been created in Minnesota
simply by adhering to NWRO's organizing guidelines.
The fact that MWRO's actual organization was a good
deal more flexible suggests that decision-makers,

i.e. the staff, intuitively realized that such a
formal organization would have been too cumbersome
for the quick decisions which often had to be made
and would have increased the possibility of interference by the members with the staff's control of
the organization.

Just before the furniture campaign was to begin,
however, internal organizational problems surfaced
at a meeting of all the Executive Committees. The
issues were: (1) whether the staff or the welfare
mothers were to control the organization and make
key decisions; and (2) the increasingly open hostility between the AFDC League and MWRO. In order to
resolve the first problem, Tina Czernek by-passed
the formal bureaucratic channel for resolving disputes through the National Coordinating Committee
and, instead, called the NWRO office in Washington,
D.C. to ask that one of the national staff (Gerlach
and Hine's "traveling evangelists") be sent to
Minneapolis to attend the next meeting of MWRO.

Bruce Thomas, one of the most charismatic and experienced members of NWRO's staff was sent. He gave
an emotional speech to the women in which he decried
the power struggles between the staff and recipients
within MWRO. (Piven and Cloward have pointed out
that this was a major source of conflict within the
national organization at this time as well.) Thomas
urged the women to put aside their differences in
order to band together against outsiders who tried
to exploit them by dividing black against white or
staff against mothers. As a result of his speech,
the by-laws were unanimously amended to spell out
more clearly the duties of both officers and staff.
For example, the staff were formally defined as non-
voting participants in the organization in accordance
with NWRO policy. At the same time, the MWRO office
in Minneapolis was selected as a central clearing-
house for information in the state, although no state
organization per se was formed. Most importantly,
Thomas' speech drew the women together once more into
a united organization and enabled them to continue
their campaign against the welfare department.

A solution to the second problem of overlapping participation between members of the AFDC League and

MWRO was also discussed at this meeting. This problem was largely a result of the segmented and decentralized form of organization characteristic of the
movement as a whole in Minnesota. MWRO leaders re-
luctantly decided that participation in both organizations should be discouraged for fear that AFDC
League members might report internal MWRO squabbles
to the press, thereby making MWRO appear divided and
weak. At the same time, however, the MWRO leaders
also insisted that further public disputes between
the two groups over goals or tactics should be stren-
uously avoided in the future.

Despite the successful effort to restore unity within MWRO, participation in the group fell off after
the failure of the furniture campaign. In the fall
of 1970 a new organizing team, Leslie and Frank
Bernstein, were hired to revitalize MWRO. They immediately began to organize what they called a "new
organization" in Minnesota. They refused to acknowl-
edge the validity of the by-laws formulated during
the furniture campaign the previous year which had
limited the role of the staff and set up a central
coordinating office for MWRO. At a "gripe
session" which took place in Sam Putnam's office at
the Legal Aid Society, some of the old leaders expressed their awareness of what was happening:

Rita Jarvis: Leslie and Frank took on a lot of res-
    ponsibility when they first arrived here. Every-
    body had to go to them. If [outsiders] wanted
    anything they'd call Frank and Leslie and if
    those two didn't like what they were doing, they
    said, "No, we're not interested." They didn't
    ask the mothers. . . .

Sam Putnam: Let's face it. You're in a power game
    right now and if no other MWRO group is going
    to back you on those by-laws then they aren't
    worth anything. The by-laws don't seem to call
    for a city-wide organization and we have no
    state organization, but we ought to. Frank and
    Leslie will say that we [the women present at
    the meeting] aren't representative enough of the
    state, but then we either should form an "interim
    state organization" or some sort of council that
    meets--if it's nothing more than the chairman
    of each local. We've got to have some sort of

central direction, some means of communication
besides just through the organizers. That's
concentrating too much power in one point. It's
not only power, but it makes you very dependent
on them.

Despite complaints such as these by the more sophisticated, experienced leaders, most MWRO members did
not push for a more formal set of links between the
locals. As a result, for several months MWRO consisted of a set of isolated locals which were coordinated solely through the Bernsteins. Personal relationships between the leaders of the new locals
in Minneapolis and St. Paul were slowly beginning to
develop, however, simply as a result of their contact with one another at demonstrations and negotiating sessions during MWRO campaigns.

The conflict between the old leaders, who wished to
establish a more democratic and orderly coordination
of MWRO locals and the Bernsteins, who wished to
maintain control of the group by acting as the only
link between groups in the state, came into the open
just after a threatened ten percent reduction in
state welfare appropriations was averted. Freed from
their concern with this external issue, the welfare
mothers used the pretext of a minor dispute over
reimbursement for travel expenses to try to resolve
the larger issue of the form of the organization.
This dispute centered on whether the member of one
local was to be reimbursed from the Minneapolis bank
account or the account of her own local.

The issue was easily resolved once the leaders of all
the locals got together, but it made even the new
members of MWRO more aware of the need for closer
communication among themselves. As a result, they
insisted on holding the first city-wide meeting of
MWRO in over a year. At this meeting, it was agreed
that regular monthly meetings must be held to plan
and coordinate campaigns, to increase the flow of
information between locals, and to settle conflicts
before they reached a crisis point. The exact formal
status of these city-wide meetings was never settled,
however. Sometimes the meetings were called joint
sessions of each local's Executive Committee; at
other times, they were called a City Executive Council.

At this same meeting the recipient leaders demanded that the Bernsteins bring all the officers of the St. Paul and Minneapolis locals together for joint planning sessions before campaigns were begun. As a result of these increased personal contacts, the welfare mothers regained a measure of control over the decision-making process and MWRO was again linked by personal ties between recipients. Although a search was started for a central MWRO office on the border between Minneapolis and St. Paul, a suitable site was never found, and coordination of statewide activities continued largely on an informal (although more frequent) basis.

Within a few months, however, participation in MWRO fell off rapidly. Due to this drop in membership, several locals disbanded and those women who wished to remain active in MWRO had to go to other neighborhoods in order to attend meetings. By the fall of 1971, MWRO was no longer a viable organization on any level. The Bernsteins had left the state for a job organizing unemployed workers on the East Coast and all that remained was a loose network of welfare mothers who, while still characterizing themselves as MWRO members, did grievance work and accepted speaking engagements purely on an individual basis.

The Welfare Mothers Movement: Direct Action, MRA, NWRO

The foregoing material on the AFDC League and MWRO illustrates the segmentary and decentralized yet reticulate nature of organizations within the Welfare Mothers Movement in Minnesota. This type of loose structure facilitated the expansion of these groups into new areas in the state, and the segmentation of existing groups into small neighborhood cells which made participation by welfare mothers feasible and more personally rewarding. The flexible nature of movement organization also enabled movement groups to contract when conditions changed and participation in a particular cell dropped off.

This type of segmented, decentralized and reticulate organization was found to be characteristic of the Welfare Mothers Movement as a whole, as well as of the local groups within the movement. The movement seen in its entirety was similar to a network in which each group was linked to others on the local or national level through overlapping participation, through personal ties between leaders, and by large public actions, such as testifying at legislative hearings or attending national conventions (see Figure 3).

For example, links between the AFDC League and Direct Action Recipients of Welfare were largely based on overlapping participation and personal ties between the leaders of the two groups. After Direct Action was founded in 1968, a number of AFDC League members who were interested in taking more militant action on welfare issues were drawn into the group. The status of Direct Action vis-a-vis the AFDC League was not particularly well defined, however. In particular, the degree of independence and autonomy of Direct Action varied according to whether the informant felt her major allegiance lay with the AFDC League or with Direct Action. Members more strongly committed to Direct Action described the group not only as independent of the AFDC League, but also often in opposition to it because of the earlier group's emphasis on conventional tactics. AFDC League participants, on the other hand, tended to describe Direct Action as an affiliate of the AFDC League and made repeated attempts to bind it closely to the larger group. For example, after several women who were involved in both groups were elected officers of the AFDC League, Direct Action was allowed to use the AFDC League membership lists for mailings as a way of "keeping the two groups coordinated." It was interesting that some outsiders less familiar with the movement perceived the relationship between the two groups in the same way as committed AFDC League members. Thus Direct Action was described as subordinate to or a part of the AFDC League, and on several occasions Direct Action's successful clothing and utilities campaigns were attributed to the AFDC League's efforts.

A year later when MWRO began organizing in Minneapolis, a similar reticulating process took place between MWRO and Direct Action. Welfare mothers in Direct Action formed the recruiting nucleus for MWRO and after Direct Action split into two

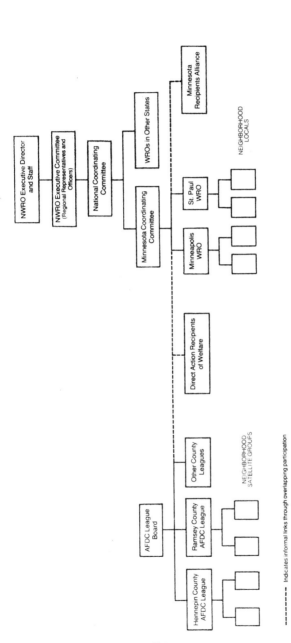

Fig. 3—The Organization of the Welfare Mothers Movement in Minnesota, 1969-72

NWRO Executive Director and Staff

NWRO Executive Committee (Regional Representatives and Officers)

National Coordinating Committee

WROs in Other States

Minnesota Coordinating Committee

Minnesota Recipients Alliance

NEIGHBORHOOD LOCALS

St. Paul WRO

Minneapolis WRO

Direct Action Recipients of Welfare

AFDC League Board

Hennepin County AFDC League

Ramsey County AFDC League

Other County Leagues

NEIGHBORHOOD SATELLITE GROUPS

-------- Indicates informal links through overlapping participation factions, those interested in continuing with welfare rights activity maintained their membership in an MWRO local. In addition, these women served as indirect links between the remaining active AFDC League members and MWRO groups during the early days of MWRO's existence, when hostility between the two groups was at its peak.

Despite the competition which was apparent, particularly in AFDC League/MWRO relations, a few welfare mothers saw some benefit from the continual proliferation of groups within the movement. Although they admitted that some conflict was selfish in motive and due to resentment at losing control over the goals and tactics of the movement, they also suggested that competition heightened their own sense of commitment. As one AFDC League leader pointed out, old members of the AFDC League became active in the group again because they disagreed with MWRO's tactics and militancy. Then she added, "MWRO keeps us honest [i.e., actively pursuing welfare issues] , although we don't tell outsiders that." Less than a year later, in fact, the leaders of the AFDC League and MWRO contacted each other in order to form an alliance to lobby jointly at the state legislature against any reduction in welfare spending in Minnesota. Clearly political unity was brought about largely as a response to external opposition from an institution which could dramatically affect the lives of all welfare recipients, regardless of the movement group of which they were a member. As is typical of movements, however, this was a temporary alliance which served to clarify both the existence of continued cleavages (i.e., MWRO and the AFDC League as separate organizations) as well as the common goals within the movement.

Finally, the Welfare Mothers Movement achieved a measure of national coordination through the organization and activities of NWRO. According to a formal organization chart distributed by NWRO, state WROs were to be linked in two ways with the national-level organization. Each state elected one NCC representative and one alternate to the National Coordinating Committee (NCC)--the decision-making body for NWRO. At the committee's quarterly meetings, NCC representatives had an opportunity to exchange information and decide the course of the national organization for the next several months. In addition, each section of the country had its own "regional representative" who served along with the officers elected at national conventions on the National Executive Committee. This body was to help plan and implement the policy decisions reached by the National Coordinating Committee in the interim between meetings of that group. The yearly NWRO conventions not only linked formally affiliated state WRO groups, but also exposed the many independent groups which attended (such as Direct Action in 1968) to NWRO ideology.

A number of informal ways of coordinating WRO groups grew up alongside this formal set of links. In many instances these unofficial linkages were more efficient and more frequently used than the official channels. For example, although contact between NWRO and each state organization ideally was to take place through the NCC representative or by direct mailings from the NWRO office, such mailings were invariably late. If quick information was needed for planning or executing a campaign, a local MWRO staff member (and occasionally recipient leaders) usually telephoned organizers in other states or in the national office with whom they were acquainted. The NWRO staff also acted as "traveling evangelists"--going around the country to WRO groups and extra-movement organizations, gathering information, coordinating activities, settling conflicts (as Bruce Thomas did for MWRO), and in general revitalizing groups for renewed efforts in confronting the welfare system.

Piven and Cloward state that the collapse of national coordination through NWRO marked the end of the Welfare Mothers Movement. This review of the movement as a whole in Minnesota, however, suggests that this was a premature judgment. Although MWRO did disappear as an organization, a few MWRO leaders, along with many welfare mothers who had never been involved in the movement before, founded a new group--the Minnesota Recipients Alliance (MRA). This organization carried on the welfare struggle for three more years, although focusing exclusively on local welfare problems once again (as had the earlier AFDC League and Direct Action).

Thus the segmentary, decentralized, yet reticulate

77

organization of the movement proved to be suffi-
ciently flexible to adapt to changes in the political environment (e.g., fluctuations in membership and in external support) which might have
caused the complete destruction of a formal or bureaucratically structured movement. From this perspective, the disappearance of MWRO and the appearance of new groups such as MRA represents not a
"failure," but an adaptive response--a retrenchment
to the local level--at a time when the national
political climate was becoming increasingly hostile
to militant activities not only by welfare mothers
but by other social movement groups as well. As
Jenkins (1979:226) points out, Piven and Cloward
might not have reached their pessimistic assessment
of the Welfare Mothers Movement if they had used a
broader approach to the study of social movements,
such as that proposed by Gerlach and Hine:

> If one accepts the model put forward by Gerlach
> and Hine (1970), movements are by their nature
> complex, polycentric, largely informally struc-
> tured operations. Half of the problem lies in
> the fact that Piven and Cloward draw on too
> narrow a conception of organization. . . . If
> there is anything we have learned in moving
> beyond the conventional wisdom of the 1950s, it
> is that movements are far more complex than
> the classic charismatic leader-devoted follower
> relationship.

Piven and Cloward's misreading of the type of organization which was characteristic of Welfare Mothers
Movement groups was thus a result not only of their
narrow and culture-bound definition of organization,
but also of their focus on the national-level political goals of a single organization, which was in
actuality only part of a larger movement. Rather
than consigning organization to the category of a
tactical mistake, the Gerlach-Hine model hypothesizes
that organization is a crucial aspect of movement
dynamics. By characterizing a social movement as a
network, their approach leads the observer beyond
the form of any one group to an analysis of the
structure and interactions of a wide variety of
organizations on both the local and national
levels.

Internal Political Processes

As has been pointed out, both the movement as a whole
and the groups within it were found to have a decentralized or polycephalous ("many-headed") organization. In other words, no single group such as NWRO
could speak for all groups engaged in welfare reform
on the local level, nor did any of the local leaders
completely agree on tactics or goals. Leaders were
unable to make decisions binding on all participants
in the movement and even had little ability to command compliance within their own organization or
segment of the movement, much less to issue orders
for the entire movement (Gerlach & Hine, 1970:36).

This type of leadership and the style of politics
characteristic of the Welfare Mothers Movement in
Minnesota were largely the result of three factors.
First and foremost was the segmentary and reticulate
nature of movement organization. In other words,
groups which saw themselves as largely autonomous
and equal cells within a larger movement (and which
were only loosely coordinated through overlapping
participation, personal friendships and infrequent
contacts through traveling evangelists or unifying
events) were extremely unlikely to develop strong
leaders who would remain unchallenged by those around
them. Second, the political process characteristic
of Welfare Mothers Movement groups was heavily influenced by the ideology of the movement (cf. Barkan,
1979 for a similar point about the feminist and antinuclear movements). All movement organizations were
committed to actualizing the American belief in
democracy: "The poor had a right to run their own
organizations and to determine their own policies"
(Piven & Cloward, 1977:284). In practice this meant
that even rank and file members were encouraged to
participate in all phases of the political process
within their groups, and those who showed the ability
and inclination to fill them were urged to assume
leadership positions. Elitism was to be avoided at
all costs. Finally, as Gerlach and Hine (1970:xiv)
point out, many social movements not only develop
within the context of a changing society, but by
their very nature, contribute to the acceleration of
change within at least some segments of that society.
It is in just such contexts of uncertainty and change

that disagreement about the proper rules of political behavior tend to be the most prevalent. When new resources or groups enter the political arena, messages about relative strength, willingness to bargain, and other kinds of actions are very likely to be misread by both sides (Bailey, 1969:179-80).

These three factors--the type of organization characteristic of the Welfare Mothers Movement, its ideology, and the context of political and social change--inevitably had an impact on the politics of movement groups, particularly: (1) the form of leadership; (2) the way in which decisions were reached; (3) the sources and frequency of conflict; and (4) the way in which conflict was resolved. Despite the loose structure and fluid political situation within the movement, a few general patterns or "rules" of politics did emerge from observation of the AFDC League and MWRO. Many of these patterns were similar for both groups, although they often differed in emphasis. The AFDC League, however, was no longer a viable organization at the time of my fieldwork and much of my information on that group comes from interviews; political activities were more fully documented for MWRO, whose meetings and behind-the-scenes politicking I was able to observe.

Leaders and officers. At some point in their existence, both the AFDC League and MWRO had by-laws which described the duties of officers in ways which did not depart significantly from those traditionally assigned those positions in American voluntary associations. This formal charter gave the appearance to outsiders of the stable, centralized structure characteristic of establishment organizations. As Jenkins (1979:226) points out, however, few organizations, much less social movement organizations, have ever been run on the basis of ideal bureaucratic rules. Scattered throughout the text describing the history and organization of the movement have been references to leaders' lack of control over their organization, and conflict between groups wishing to maintain their independence. Often internal politics proceeded almost as if the formal rules embodied in the by-laws did not exist, as these organizationally unsophisticated welfare mothers sought to define in their own way the appropriate activities of "leaders," "officers," and "staff." A measure of stability and common expectations about the appropriate behavior assigned to these three roles ultimately did emerge, however, due in large part to the efforts of a long-term staff person, leader, or core of committed participants to develop a set of unwritten political customs for dealing with recurrent issues or problems.

Leaders in the AFDC League and MWRO were ordinarily very competent, although not necessarily well-educated women who were capable of taking strong stands if necessary against members of the established order. The normative rules about leadership within both organizations,[3] however, stressed that leaders were weak, had little decision-making authority (which was invested in the membership), and lacked sanctions to enforce the decisions which were reached. For example, MWRO participants suggested that leaders had two main tasks: (1) "getting the mothers in-volved," which included recruiting new members and maintaining the interest of old members by inform-ing them about organization events and gossip; and (2) "getting things for the mothers," by writing pro-posals for funding, making contacts with influential people in the larger society, and leading demonstra-tions or grievance actions. Only three of the most active and sophisticated leaders included the plan-ning of group activities as one of the leader's tasks. In actuality, most of the planning of cam-paign goals and strategy did fall pragmatically to the staff. For this reason, the staff and not the recipient leaders were held responsible for the suc-cess or failure of MWRO's campaigns.

Even in carrying out the limited activities actually expected of them, the leaders in Welfare Mothers Movement groups had to rely primarily on persuasion rather than commands. As one AFDC League member pointed out, leaders in that group could not be au-thoritarian in their behavior because "the women did not want another social worker telling them what to do." In the same vein, MWRO leaders suggested that in their group, "leaders were supposed to be follow-ers and do what the mothers say."

Women with leadership qualities tended to move into the available formal offices in the organizations,

but not always. For example, one of the founders of
the AFDC League stated that, "The opinion leaders
didn't have to hold office because people called
them and if the opinion leaders wanted something
done they would call others to discuss it--they could
get people to do what they wanted." The general
tendency in the development of these groups, however,
was for greater influence to shift towards those
holding legitimate offices as the majority of members
became more experienced in the organization--usually
about a year after the group had been founded. This
was the case with the AFDC League where by-laws were
written up in early 1967, a little over a year after
the major proliferation of AFDC League county and
satellite groups had occurred. Since these by-laws
invariably specified that decisions were to be made
by majority vote, more of the political process
moved out into the open at this time.

Both formal and informal leaders, however, relied
heavily on developing a consensus of opinion among
the key members of their groups before bringing an
issue out in the open for a public vote at meetings.
By telephoning members in order to sound out their
opinions, leaders were able to gauge the feelings
of their members and at the same time apply pressure
and gather support for their position on an issue
away from the public eye. Such a process also allowed
for the development of compromises at an early point
in the decision-making process, thereby minimizing
open conflict at meetings. Not all leaders were
equally capable of using these informal political
rules skillfully, however, and others used the existence of this covert process as a weapon against
existing leaders by labelling it as "corruption."

A good example of the constraints on movement leaders
was the role of the State AFDC League Board president.
The state president was to direct and implement legislative activities and maintain contact between
county groups during and between legislative sessions.
Much of the actual cooperation between groups, however, was the result of this woman's skill in gathering support and developing a consensus among the
leaders of each group. Such skill was especially
crucial in interactions between the two largest
county groups in Minneapolis and St. Paul, which

tended to be jealous of any attempt by the other to unduly influence AFDC League affairs. Thus one woman who had been state president told me that she was elected as a "compromise candidate" who was acceptable to both these county groups because of her close personal ties with many of the leaders in both cities. In spite of this, however, she stated that she had often been the focus of conflict, which she attributed to her lack of "charisma." While this may have been a contributing factor, her position as the main link between basically autonomous and sometimes competitive AFDC League groups which had to cooperate in order to achieve their common goals also contributed to her problems.

There were not only difficulties inherent in the positions of the leaders who linked segments of the movement, however, but also opportunities, as will be seen in the following section.

The role of staff members in movement groups. As was pointed out above, Piven and Cloward (1977:284-5) have stated that the emphasis on control of WRO groups by the recipients themselves led to a situation in which organizers and other staff members could engage in only two types of activities in their role as outsiders in a poor people's organization:

> First, they should act as staff, subordinating themselves to policymaking bodies composed exclusively of the poor. As staff, they would contribute their technical skills to the work of the organization. They would, for example, provide information on the technical aspects of various issues with which the organization was dealing--in this case, the extremely complex rules and regulations of the welfare system. They would also run training programs in methods for dealing with the welfare bureaucracy--how to negotiate with welfare officials, or how to organize demonstrations. Second, they would cultivate those with leadership potential, tutoring them in techniques of leadership in the expectation that the role of the organizer would wither away. This is the model that NWRO and most of the local WROs subsequently came to espouse.

Thus Piven and Cloward (1977:285) contend that organizers were totally subordinate to the recipient members to the point of being barred from attending meetings at national conventions where elected leaders from the various state organizations established overall policy for NWRO. Gossip at the NWRO Convention in 1971, however, gave a different picture of the situation, at least at the local level. Many delegates were complaining that the organizers in their states actually had too much power and were continually attempting to manipulate the decision-making process within their groups.

The activities outlined above by Piven and Cloward provide an accurate description of the normatively appropriate role for staff members associated with both MWRO and the AFDC League. The actual behavior of the staff, however, did not always approach this ideal (although it did more so in the AFDC League than in MWRO). As could be expected, welfare mothers and staff members described and justified the discrepancy between their ideal and real behavior in different ways.

Most AFDC League members credited June Waldheim with having played the correct role as the group's advisor who was ready with services, information, and suggestions if the women requested them. In addition, June had a fairly neutral position as staff person for all the satellite groups in Minneapolis, while acting as staff for the state organization as well. As a result, she stated that she was often called upon to act as a go-between and mediate conflicts within satellite groups or between county organizations. June described this as the role of a "supportive servant," who smoothed the feelings of leaders who had suffered a defeat or a personal affront and were threatening to quit the organization. Some members of the AFDC League, however, complained that June later began to assume a more active role in the group than she had when it was first founded. One woman recounted an instance in which June had reimbursed a member for travel expenses without first having asked the members' permission--"just like some social worker in disguise." June agreed that she had not taken as active a role in the AFDC League initially because of the demands of her job at the YWCA and because she knew little about the welfare system at that time. From June's point of view, her increased involvement in the running of the organization was forced on her by the continual turnover in leadership which the AFDC League experienced in its later years. For this reason, she was often the only one who knew what to do or where to get information when action on some problem was needed.

Within MWRO, the staff (composed of a salaried organizer and a volunteer staff of students and anti-poverty workers) were supposed to conform to the ideal role outlined above as well. In addition to these normative activities, however, observation of MWRO suggested that the staff: (1) provided emotional support for the welfare mothers in their dealings with powerful individuals and institutions in the larger society (similar to June's supportive servant role); and (2) from the outset pragmatically assumed a major leadership role in the organization. The different experience of the AFDC League and MWRO in regard to the prominence of the staff in the decision-making process stemmed from several sources.

First, whereas June Waldheim had little knowledge about the welfare system initially, both MWRO organizers had had previous experience with it. Tina Czernek had been a recipient and Leslie Bernstein had just received a master's degree in social work/community organizing, and both women had worked with WRO groups elsewhere in the country before coming to Minnesota. Second, the AFDC League quickly developed a working set of links between segments of the group through institutionalized, regular meetings and through the personal ties between leaders. MWRO locals, however, tended to remain isolated one from another with the staff providing the major linkages between segments. Third, the goals and strategy of the two groups affected the role of staff members. According to Carl Jones, Sam Putnam, and several of the staff members who worked for the group, the staff planned MWRO's campaign strategy at closed staff meetings and then manipulated the recipient leaders into supporting staff decisions. Many of the staff stated they believed this was necessary because they feared that, if left to their own devices, the mothers would prefer a strategy based on private meetings and negotiations with the welfare department. This strategy would have been similar to that selected by AFDC League members and contrary to the public militancy advocated by NWRO leaders. Voting at MWRO meetings then amounted to little more than a ratification of decisions which had been made elsewhere.

Both organizers in MWRO also managed to maintain a position of pragmatic leadership by controlling the flow of information from the larger society into the group. Thus they could limit the alternatives presented to the mothers as feasible or proper courses of action--often expressed as a choice between "demonstrating" or "doing nothing." The organizers and staff also attempted to gather their own support group in the form of a faction of loyal supporters in order to defeat the proposals of other leaders which differed from their own. For example, Tina managed to avoid any open questioning of her leadership of MWRO until the beginning of the furniture campaign in 1970. Not only did the welfare mothers lack experience in running organizations, but also Tina was particularly adroit at using the fact that she had been on welfare, was a mother herself, and a former member of a WRO group to turn aside criticism of her actions. As one leader put it later, "Tina was like a government." Carl Jones made a similar point when he said:

> Tina had much more an ability than I did in the dramatics and how to plan a demonstration and how to organize the mothers. She did it beautifully and the mothers recognized this, and they respected her for this kind of leadership and authority which she could assert.

In addition, Tina was continually on the phone or visiting MWRO locals around the city passing on information, getting input on issues, and persuading key leaders to support her decisions. She did provide an important service linking MWRO locals into a more cohesive organization this way, although the end result was to enhance her control of the group. Many participants recognized that Tina had overstepped the limits of her role as organizer, but they were willing to forgive many of her actions after she left Minneapolis.

When Leslie Bernstein and her husband began organizing in Minnesota, they ran into immediate strong opposition from a core of old leaders who had remained in the MWRO group. In fact, however, the Bernsteins actually manipulated the organization less openly than had Tina. As Sam Putnam said:

> The Bernsteins very unconsciously run this organization. I've heard a lot of allegations about how the Northside local is together, but the leaders depend on Leslie. I don't know because I don't spend much time up there myself, but I wouldn't doubt that might be the case. I've been to meetings on the Northside where it has been as much spoonfeeding as anything else. It's just that that area was never organized before. If somebody doesn't have a bitter taste in their mouth it's much easier to organize them. If you talk about the organization in terms of purpose and process--right now the Bernsteins are too hung up on purpose. They keep talking about organizing the state, but somehow they're not holding the existing organization together. What's the reason for it? I don't think the mothers think it's their organization. They don't feel a part of it. Once you get that proprietary interest in the organization--well, that's why last year [when Tina was organizer] they had such incredible hassles. Even when they were hassling, the ladies at least felt that it was their organization. That was one way that Tina could relate to the ladies that Frank and Leslie can't.

The Bernsteins were openly criticized in part because by late 1970 MWRO's experienced leaders were more confident of their abilities and willing to challenge an organizer's attempt to manipulate the group. Leslie also antagonized the old leaders by forming what she called a "new" organization in Minnesota. She attempted to ease out the women who had held MWRO together over the summer of 1970 and discouraged old supporters such as Carl Jones and Sam Putnam-- both of whom had strong ties with the previous leaders--from attending meetings. Leslie also failed to develop an informal communication network within MWRO as Tina had, and refused to hold regular citywide meetings where open discussion could occur and personal relationships could be formed between new and old MWRO leaders. In addition, Leslie had never been on welfare and, in fact, rarely made use of the normative themes which were available to her (e.g., such as publicly emphasizing she was "trying to work herself out of a job") to allay criticism.

MWRO members who had been involved in the group the year before tended to see Leslie's actions as another attempt to reassert staff control and to get the women to rubber-stamp staff decisions. Newer members did not believe that Leslie consciously was trying to play one group off against the other, but they also felt that she had not pushed as hard as she could have for the establishment of clear lines of communication between the locals in Minneapolis. When asked to comment on these charges during an interview, Leslie claimed that some of the leaders from the Northside locals had specifically requested that citywide meetings not be held. They had disliked the quarreling at MWRO meetings while Tina was the organizer, and so preferred not to have any joint meetings where conflict might erupt. Some doubt is cast on the strength of this feeling among Northside leaders, however, by their later eagerness to establish regular joint meetings with the other MWRO locals in 1971. Regardless of the reason, the lack of citywide meetings (as well as of meetings between the Minneapolis and St. Paul WROs) did effectively isolate locals from one another and worked to Leslie's advantage. Her strongest criticism came from the experienced Southside members, whereas the Northside locals were for the most part made up of previously unorganized recipients who usually supported Leslie's suggestions or her position in a conflict. After joint meetings began and after the Northside leaders had more exposure to other WRO leaders at NWRO conventions, however, many of them reported being disillusioned with organizers in general, and with Leslie in particular.

This material on the activities of leaders and organizers in Minnesota provides an interesting contrast to Piven and Cloward's (1977:310-11) assessment of what they describe as the problem of entrenched leadership in WRO groups:

The elaboration of organization meant the
elaboration of leadership positions on the
neighborhood, city, and state levels. Once
groups had formed and affiliated with NWRO and
leaders had been duly elected, these leadership
positions became a source of intense preoccupation and competition. . . . These circumstances
constrained the expansion of membership, for
the leaders came to have an investment in membership stasis. Recipient leaders at all levels
of the organization had to be periodically re-
elected; new members represented a threat.
Struggles for leadership succession might ensue;
existing leaders might be toppled. . . . Con-
sequently leaders resisted new membership organizing ventures. . . and [resisted] organizing
recipients from other relief categories, such
as the aged and working poor.

One solution to this problem according to Piven and
Cloward, was to have organizers form new groups
without the cooperation of recipient leaders and
then precipitate power confrontations which would
force old leaders out of office or out of the group
altogether. The Bernsteins attempted to make use of
this solution in Minnesota by refusing to accept the
validity of the old by-laws and by forming a "new"
organization. It was, unfortunately, a solution
without a problem.

While entrenched leaders may have posed problems on
the national level or in other states, in Minnesota
access to leadership by new members did not appear
to be blocked. For one thing, leadership positions
(and offices) were regularly opened up when new neighborhood locals were formed--which tended to be a con-
tinuous process in Minnesota. Even in the established
locals, the elected officers readily accepted new
members who were capable and willing to work into the
informal leadership network or suggested they run
for office. For example, in 1971 a new office, that
of Sergeant-at-Arms, was created to accommodate a
woman who wished to become more involved in MWRO.
In fact, whatever role which experienced leaders had
in running the organization was not due primarily to
their own maneuvering, but to the reluctance of most
MWRO members to take a public leadership role even
when it was offered them. Many of the welfare mothers

did not wish to spend the time that holding an
office required, feared harassment from people
opposed to welfare if their names were reported in
the news media as an officer of a movement group,
or they wished to avoid the conflict and embarrassment which often accompanied interactions across
class and sex boundaries with politicians and welfare officials (Hertz, 1980).

Decision-making. As was apparent in the discussion
of the activities of the leaders and staff of Welfare
Mothers Movement groups, a great deal of the decision-
making process often occurred outside the formal
context of meetings. Meetings were by no means dull
affairs, however, for some decisions were genuinely
made at these times, and it was in the context of
public meetings that changes in the internal power
structure became apparent.

The by-laws of both the AFDC League and MWRO specified that meetings were to be conducted according to
parliamentary procedure. Many meetings were, however, a great deal more informal. While the welfare
mothers involved in these movement groups had not
had a great deal of experience in other voluntary
associations, they were, nevertheless, well aware of
what was "proper," i.e., majority voting, the making
of motions, and recording the minutes were valued as
the business-like way of conducting a meeting. Most
women lamented the fact that meetings were often
"disorganized" and interrupted by arguments about
what they saw as "petty" issues. (The only exception
to this general sentiment was expressed by an MWRO
member--a black woman who had previously been involved
in a Civil Rights group. She opposed parliamentary
procedure on the grounds that "those were the rules
that kept you poor in the first place.") Despite
this commitment to formal procedure and majority
voting, however, many decisions were reached through
the development of consensus among those attending
a meeting.

For Americans, it often comes as a surprise that most
of the world's peoples have tended to emphasize consensual decision-making and compromise over the kind
of public confrontation and the magnification of differences required by our practice of reaching decisions through majority votes. When decisions are

made on the basis of consensus, however, no action can be taken that is not consented to by every participant. If anyone dissents from a decision, discussion must continue until everyone finally agrees, or at least agrees to stand aside and allow the group to reach a decision despite the absence of total consensus (Wasserman, 1977, quoted in Barkan, 1979:29). The women involved in Welfare Mothers Movement groups, however, believed that decisions reached by majority vote and proper parliamentary procedure were more legitimate than those reached by consensus. For example, their commitment to the normative American pattern of voting was so strong that even when votes were not taken and decisions actually reached by consensus, participants sometimes later described the issue as having been voted on.

An understanding of why decisions were reached in one or another of these two ways requires a closer look at the conduct of meetings in MWRO between 1969 and 1971. Factors other than just values influenced the methods of making decisions: (1) the segmentary, decentralized nature of movement organization; (2) the life cycle of the organization; (3) the size and frequency of interaction within the group; and (4) the focus of the group's task (i.e., on internal affairs or on external issues against which the group must present itself as a unified body (Bailey, 1968: 1-20).

First, the Welfare Mothers Movement was composed of semiautonomous, decentralized segments with weak leaders who could not issue orders, make binding decisions, or enforce sanctions against participants who did not go along with group decisions. Welfare mothers who disagreed with a decision often simply stopped participating in the group for a time. The leaders' inability to command compliance with decisions, even if they were reached as a result of a vote by the majority, inevitably led them to ensure continued participation by attempting to compromise and develop a consensus of opinion among members. In addition to the pattern of leadership, the size and stage in the life cycle of the organization affected the decision-making process. When locals were first formed, meetings were usually well attended, often involving upwards of 100 women who rarely knew one another. As Bailey suggests, decision-making by majority vote in

our society tends to predominate in just such large
groups which interact infrequently (or whose members have never interacted at all before).   Thus
parliamentary procedure tended to be more rigidly
adhered to following the formation of large new
groups of unacquainted women. As the groups matured
and attendance dropped off, decision-making tended
to rely more heavily on the achievement of consensus
and often even voice votes were not called for.
Finally, the focus of the organization also affected
the type of decision-making, for it was at the height
of the campaigns when MWRO groups were most unified
in their opposition to the welfare department or
other institution that decisions were most often
reached by consensus rather than voting.

Frequently discussions were long and meandering, with
plenty of opportunity for all present to get a feeling for the general sentiment of the participants.
Even close observation failed to make clear exactly
what decisions had been reached, thus allowing greater latitude in subsequent actions by the leaders.
For example, if a consensus of opinion was reached
and then a decision later became a source of contention, it could be dismissed as a "mistake" if no
clear vote had been taken and recorded. A compromise
could then be worked out and opponents of the original decision could continue their active participation in MWRO without hard feelings.

In other words, although from an outsider's point of
view movement meetings may often have seemed chaotic
and indecisive, from a different perspective these
qualities provided a number of benefits for movement
groups. The alternation between voting and consensual
decision-making was not simply random, nor due solely to a lack of organizational experience on the part
of the welfare mothers. Rather the use of one form
or another was closely connected with factors such
as the decentralized nature of movement leadership,
the focus of the group on internal or external issues,
and the desire of the women to restrain open conflict
in order to maintain close personal ties and achieve
movement goals. Thus the use of consensual decision-
making has psychological, organizational, and tactical benefits: it is a way of involving all meeting
participants in the decision-making process, leads
to good morale, minimizes feelings of resentment or

coercion by the group, may possibly reduce hostility and factionalism within the movement, and heightens participants' commitment to final decisions on goals and strategy (Barkan, 1979:30).

Conflict and its resolution. Open conflict is inevitable in all groups, whatever efforts participants may make to avoid it. Conflict surfaced most dramatically within Welfare Mothers Movement groups immediately preceding or following campaigns--whether that involved lobbying at the legislature for the AFDC League or demonstrations at the welfare department for MWRO. The timing of these outbreaks of conflict resulted from the general tension surrounding these events, the need for increased interaction and cooperation between local groups, leaders, and staff in order to successfully conduct a major political action, and the lack of a critical need to unite against a common enemy at that precise point in time (this was especially true after the completion of a campaign).

Several examples have been given of conflicts which were the result of competition between neighborhood-level groups or county groups over their autonomy of action or control of financial resources. This kind of conflict resulted largely from the segmentary and decentralized nature of movement organization. A more frequent source of conflict within MWRO arose from the contradiction between the normative rule that the mothers were to control the organization and the continuing pragmatic domination of the staff. This kind of conflict was conducted through the development of factions.

As Gerlach and Hine (1973:171) point out, "If there is anything that is generally decried by observers and participants alike, it is the factionalism that is almost a hallmark of movements." We tend to believe that movements succeed "in spite of" factions and internal discord, or fail because of them. In point of fact, there are two ways of interpreting conflict found in the social science literature: it can be viewed as having positive functions in the maintenance of a group (e.g. by allowing people to "let off steam,") or it can be seen as having negative maladaptive consequences (e.g., by paralyzing groups so they are unable to act in concert to achieve their goals) (LeVine, 1961:3).

93

The former interpretation is the point of view
adopted here. As Bailey (1969:52) suggests, we
should ignore the pejorative connotations of the
word, "factions," and look dispassionately at the
circumstances in which factional alignments emerge
cross-culturally. From this perspective the process
is not at all frivolous, but is somewhat like adoles-
cence. Factions represent a rejection of past alle-
giances and a fumbling and (to outsiders and some
participants) occasionally selfish searching for new
ways of arranging social interactions. Factions
tend to arise, therefore, in the context of change
when some new kind of political resource appears which
existing groups cannot exploit. In other words,
the sole reason for the existence of factions is
political dispute over control of resources (in
spite of whatever other rationalizations may be offered by participants). The goal is not to drive
people away, however, but to continually show through
small confrontations which leader is most able or
which group the strongest (Bailey, 1969:88-91;
Nicholas, 1968:27-30).

These features of factions were indeed reflected in
the factions which appeared in MWRO. A number of
factional showdowns took place within MWRO over
what initially seemed to be unimportant issues, but
which actually were triggered by the more serious
dispute over the control of the organization. The
persistence of this underlying conflict in spite
of the variety of minor issues which were publicly
identified as the problem explains a feature of factional conflict which is often puzzling to observers.
As Bailey (1969:52) points out, faction members may
take different sides on the same issue at different
points in time, with a "cavalier disregard for the
ideological consistency of the causes." For example,
the faction within MWRO which was led by Rita Jarvis
often tried to undermine support for the Bernsteins
either by complaining that Leslie was doing too much
and "trying to take over the organization" or else
that the Bernsteins did not work hard enough for the
salary they received while making the mothers do
everything.

While factional conflict during Leslie's year as
organizer was as bitter as that under Tina, it was
also more easily and quickly contained. In large

part this was because MWRO members had developed a customary set of redressive mechanisms which could be brought to bear on disputes before they became public or could lessen the severity of open conflict once it had occurred. The redressive mechanisms which kept conflict to an acceptable level in MWRO so that it could coordinate activities and unite for campaigns included several techniques or processes already described: (1) temporary withdrawal from active participation by a member; (2) withdrawal and the formation of a new movement group (which may have had negative consequences for the original organization but potentially positive ones for the movement as a whole); (3) portrayal of earlier opposition as the result of a misunderstanding; (4) maneuvering outsiders into a position in which they, and not members, could be blamed for precipitating conflicts; (5) collusion to table controversial issues (even if a vote had already been taken) or to call for a re-vote if it became apparent that significant opposition to an issue existed; and (6) periodic gripe sessions as a way of letting off steam and trying to reach a compromise before conflict erupted at a public meeting.

In addition, what can be called internal intermediaries were used to settle conflicts between individuals and groups. The individuals who mediated in this way held neutral positions vis-a-vis their Welfare Mothers Movement group--or as Tuden (1966: 281) has put it, were "disengaged from the web of affiliations" because they were not identified with any single individual or group. June Waldheim functioned in this capacity for the AFDC League. Sam Putnam, the Legal Aid lawyer, and Carl Jones were the two individuals who acted as intermediaries within MWRO.

For example, Jones had been associated with MWRO since it was founded in 1969 and helped organize an auxiliary group of supporters for MWRO called the Friends of Welfare Rights. He described himself as a "street minister" who was hired by a Southside church to minister to the spiritual needs of community members who did not attend church regularly. While Carl Jones had no authority within MWRO as a result of his position as chair of the Friends group, he did enjoy close personal relationships with both the organizers and most of the mothers. He was particularly effective

in settling conflicts because of his religious role.
He described his influence with MWRO in this way:

> I carry authority with me simply because I have
> a tendency to be a male chauvinist and assert
> some authority. I'm vocal, I have a position,
> I have a religion and many of the mothers--even
> though they may not actively participate in it--
> it means something to them. In their background,
> when the minister says something, it means some-
> thing to them. So I carry a whole lot of bag-
> gage along with me in terms of their view of me.
> So in that sense I have influence in the group
> and I know it.

Carl, despite his suggestion that he was a male chau-
vinist, pointed out that he had been concerned about
the manipulation of the mothers by the staff. He
claimed that he had worked hard to avoid developing
a "paternalistic" leadership role, such as he felt
Father Groppe had with Civil Rights groups in
Milwaukee. While being a man undoubtedly influenced
his interactions with the welfare mothers, it was not
a necessary prerequisite for settling conflicts,
since June Waldheim was involved in similar kinds of
activities with the AFDC League. Far more important
was their neutral structural position with the group.
An example of how Carl Jones resolved a dispute between two old leaders and two new active members
will illustrate this process.

The conflict arose when two new members of the MWRO
Steering Committee, Lila Rogers and Shelley Cook,
were offended by the profane language used by Rita
Jarvis and Elizabeth James on the way to the demonstration which was to begin a new MWRO campaign.
Lila discussed the problem with Shelley and they
agreed they might quit the organization because of
this episode. Lila hesitated to talk the matter over
directly with anyone in MWRO, but agreed to let
Shelley discuss the problem with some of her friends
in other community organizations. After calling
several people, including Leslie Bernstein (who
refused to become involved), Shelley was finally directed to Carl Jones. As a result of his conversa-
tion with Shelley, Carl took Rita out to lunch and
told her that some new mothers, Shelley in particular,
were upset about their language. Rita immediately

conferred with Elizabeth James, who called Shelley, apologized, and pointed out that any problems could be brought openly to the officers involved, rather than allowed to fester below the surface or taken to the staff. Shelley later told me that she had been very embarrassed by Elizabeth's call at the time, and had been pleasantly surprised when Rita and Elizabeth were friendly to her at the next meeting of the Steering Committee. She later realized that this episode, more than anything else, had made her feel a part of the organization. Thus Carl Jones played an important role in resolving a conflict which had threatened to split the Steering Committee just as a united front was needed to conduct an MWRO campaign. Without his availability as a go-between, the women might have dropped out. Instead, the episode heightened a new member's commitment to the organization and her feeling of personal loyalty to two of its most influential leaders.

Gerlach and Hine (1973:171) admit that factionalism and other types of internal conflict which are largely stimulated by the segmentary and decentralized form of movement organization may be drains on the energy of participants. While such discord may indeed have negative consequences on the individual level for some members, from the broader perspective of the movement as a whole, such competition and rivalry may also generate an escalation of effort and forward motion. For example, in the early conflict between the AFDC League and MWRO, differences in goals and tactics tended to increase the determination of participants to further their own ideas and recruit new members, thereby expanding the influence of the total movement.

Gerlach and Hine also suggest that a close analysis of the warring factions or groups within a movement in any one locality shows an interesting pattern. Militant elements within the movement will make outrageous demands upon the establishment, usually through some sort of disruptive activity, but are seldom rewarded directly with what they ask. Rather, representatives of the moderate or conservative segments of the movement will come forward with more reasonable requests, which suddenly look quite acceptable to harried decision-makers. Thus the very factionalism that most people view as a weakness can, as an unintended consequence, advance the interests of the movement as a whole. Precisely this situation occurred during the MWRO furniture campaign in 1970. Warned in advance by an AFDC League leader that MWRO was preparing a campaign on the issue of low furniture allotments, the welfare department decided to go ahead with the more modest raise which had previously been suggested by the AFDC League. While the welfare officials' purpose was to undercut MWRO, the end result benefited all welfare mothers in the county.

In addition to the energy enhancing function of competition between movement groups, the segmented yet reticulate structure of movement organization is adaptive in other ways as well. Such a structure permits the movement to recruit members from a broad range of social backgrounds and personality types, as was seen in the case of the Indian AFDC League or in the different goals of the women attracted to the AFDC League as opposed to MWRO or Direct Action. A third adaptive feature of this type of organization is the ability of each cell to contribute in its own way. Not only does this provide a maximum opportunity for personal involvement in any particular group, but also encourages innovation and initiative, particularly the opportunity for small-scale social innovations. As Gerlach and Hine (1973:171) state:

> Social problems are multifaceted. Even though a movement as a whole may address itself to one type of problem, such as war, the status of women, or environmental deterioration, these problems manifest themselves in different ways in different parts of the country and among different groups of people.

In Minnesota, the county AFDC League groups outside the Twin Cities were able to focus on the welfare issues of most relevance to their members (and which were often unique to their city) without the interference of a unified central organization attempting to direct change in a single way. This was, in fact, one of the problems faced by NWRO in the early 1970s (Piven & Cloward, 1977:349-50). The organization's increasing focus on national-level lobbying against FAP and its repeated calls for demonstrations in the nation's capital drew funds and recipient leaders away from local activities and problems, such as the flat grant system in Minnesota. The appearance of the Minnesota Recipients Alliance attests to the continued vitality of the movement as a whole, however, through a renewed focus on specific local problems of real personal interest to local participants.

Gerlach and Hine suggest that a fourth adaptive feature of segmented, polycephalous movement organization is the prevention or at least minimization of effective suppression or co-optation of the total movement. The duplication of effort, the self-sufficiency of most local movement groups, and the large number of actual or potential leaders make it impossible to destroy a movement by wiping out one segment or getting rid of one leader. This is very similar to a point made by Jenkins (1979:226) in his critique of Piven and Cloward's thesis. They contend that the Welfare Mothers Movement failed because poor people's organizations are particularly vulnerable to co-optation by the economic and political elite. Having pointed out that, according to the Gerlach-Hine model, movements are not bureaucracies but largely informally structured operations, Jenkins goes on to suggest that the conversion of movements into lobby organizations which may abandon insurgent goals is clearly a hazard of any kind of structure-- "but it is a decision, not an inevitability." The history of the Welfare Mothers Movement organizations in Minnesota does show cases in which individual women found jobs, were neutralized through appointment to an advisory board, or were intimidated by the threats of outsiders. As women left movement groups, however, new leaders emerged to take their place. As groups such as Direct Action disappeared, members of those groups started new organizations and recruited previously unorganized recipients to continue the struggle to achieve movement goals.

Finally, this kind of organizational structure minimizes the effect of failure, such that the loss of a campaign by one group does not affect the functioning of other independent groups, or cause the whole movement to fail. As Gerlach and Hine (1973:166-7) point out:

> Significant social change is always accompanied by change in individual behavior and attitudinal patterns. In any movement a great deal of energy

99

is expended in overt attempts to influence the
decision-making process--sometimes by conventional means ("working within the system"),
sometimes by unconventional means. These bursts
of peak-energy output are characteristically
temporary and occur at irregular intervals. But
it is a mistake to interpret the intervening ·
periods of apparent inactivity as a sign the
movement is not capable of sustained action. An
equal amount of energy, perhaps even more, is
expended on changing the individual attitudes
and behavior of both participants and potential
supporters.

This is one of the ways in which the organizational
aspect of a movement is interrelated with the factor
of ideology.

FOOTNOTES

1. This may be an unusual form of social organization for Westerners, but a number of societies organize exclusively in this way and are called "acepha-
lous" (i.e., without a head) societies.

2. The clearest example of this basis for proliferation was a satellite group in Minneapolis composed
entirely of American Indians. Several Indians who
were on welfare heard of the AFDC League's activities
and expressed interest in joining. One condition of
their affiliation, however, was that they be allowed
to form their own satellite group, to be called the
"Indian AFDC League," and that they be granted a large
measure of autonomy in planning their own activities.

3. A general distinction will be drawn throughout
this analysis between normative and pragmatic rules.
Bailey (1969:5-6) suggests that politics has its public face (normative rules) and its private wisdom
(pragmatic rules). Normative rules tend to set broad
limits to possible actions, such as implied in the con-
cepts of "honesty" or "democracy," and are used to
judge actions as ethically wrong or right. Pragmatic
rules fill the empty spaces left between the norms.
These rules recommend tactics and maneuvers not on
whether they are just or not, but on whether they are
effective.

CHAPTER 5

Ideology

One of the most recent reviews of the anthropological
literature on social and political movements chas-
tises our lack of concern with ideology and urges
social scientists to focus on the "political culture"
and symbols used by movements cross-culturally
(Nicholas, 1973). The Gerlach-Hine model does indeed
give a central place to ideology as one of the five
key factors crucial to the growth and spread of a
movement. Gerlach and Hine (1970:xvii) define
ideology in this way:

> An ideology codifies values and goals, provides
> a conceptual framework by which all experiences
> or events relative to these goals may be inter-
> preted, motivates and provides rationale for
> envisioned changes, defines the opposition, and
> forms the basis for conceptual unification of
> a segmented network of groups.

Ideologies not only unite a movement, however, they
also divide it. Any ideology is composed of a few
basic tenets shared by all groups within the movement
which provide the basis for the actual formation of
alliances. Movement ideologies also are made up of
a large number of variations on these themes. These
underlie the divergence, schisms, and factionalism
characteristic of movements (Gerlach & Hine, 1973:174).

Gerlach and Hine (1973:185-9) go on to suggest that
whatever the specific content (i.e., symbols, slogans,
etc.) of an ideology, certain generic characteristics
can be identified. These general characteristics dis-
tinguish an ideology from the system of values accepted by members of the larger society: (1) by providing a vision of a different future; (2) by giving
participants a sense of self-worth and power which is
usually at variance with the social identities previously assigned to them; (3) by rejecting the ideal-
real gap found in all human behavior, thus providing
participants with a different set of criteria by
which to judge the morality, legality, and success
of their own actions; and (4) by engendering a quality
of dogmatism or intolerance for opposing views. The

101

description of the ideology of the two main groups
within the Welfare Mothers Movement in Minnesota
will be organized in terms of these four general characteristics.

The ideology of the Welfare Mothers Movement groups
consisted of the following core of shared beliefs·
abstracted from the statements of active participants
in both the AFDC League and MWRO. First, the welfare
mothers consistently emphasized their right to self-
determination in their private lives, specifically
expressed as the right to choose between staying home
as a full-time mother or going to work. Second, the
women stated they should be treated with human dignity despite their public dependency. Finally, movement participants agreed on the importance of organizing in order to better their own lives and to influence the political process as other groups of Americans
do. These commonly held beliefs were expressed in
general terms (Gerlach and Hine call this "adaptive
ambiguity") so that each group within the movement
could "do its own thing"--whether that entailed self-
help activities, lobbying, or militant actions. Yet
at times of increased opposition from the welfare and
political systems, such as occurred in 1971 in
Minnesota when a number of reductions in welfare expenditures were proposed, the women could rise above
tactical differences to form short-term alliances
through their common commitment to these three themes.
At the same time, differences between the AFDC League
and MWRO did exist. Since idea systems do not belong
to the conceptual level alone, the variations which
did develop within the movement inevitably had an impact on the women's actual behavior, particularly on
their choice of tactics and patterns of interaction
with institutions in the larger society.

A Vision of the Future

Movement ideologies provide a vision of a future world
which is usually embodied in symbolic, easily commun-
icated terms commonly referred to as "rhetoric" or
the "party line" by outsiders. These slogans, however, enable newly recruited participants to interpret
their own personal experiences in terms of movement
ideology. Knowledge of these themes strengthens the
defenses of a new participant against criticism, and

provides patterned answers to questions raised by opponents of the movement--whose objections themselves tend to be patterned as well (Gerlach & Hine, 1973:174-5).

For the AFDC League, the vision of the future they hoped for was not so very different from the existing scheme of things. Most AFDC League members did not wish to change society so much as to alter their place in it. These women were involved in a search for social mobility, in other words, rather than social change. For example, AFDC League members genuinely believed in the real possibility of getting off welfare and moving into a more middle-class lifestyle through self-help activities, especially education. In spite of the AFDC League's public emphasis upon changing legislation, most members stated that they personally felt that self-help activities and "changing the public image of the welfare recipient" were more important to them.

This belief is similar to that of the early Civil Rights Movement and conservative blacks today. Their goal of integration is based on the "concept that blacks must earn their place in white society and is associated with the idea that blacks must take responsibility for their own inadequacy" (Gerlach & Hine, 1970:18). This statement sounds very similar to the preamble of the Hennepin County AFDC League by-laws which indicated that one of the goals of the organization was "to create awareness of the responsibilities as well as the rights of recipients." In other words, reliance upon self-help to overcome dependency implied that poor women have a large measure of control over the circumstances which ultimately led them to seek welfare, rather than being a victim of both the economic institutions and the assigned gender roles of the larger society. One result of this belief was the ultimate loss of the most capable women. As one AFDC League officer put it (Hertz, 1977:603-4):

> You can only be president of a welfare organization so long and then you have to grow. If you don't--well, it's a contradiction in terms of what your group means. . . . That's one thing about the AFDC League, it got so good it destroyed itself. Everybody really believed in self-help.

AFDC League members intellectually agreed with the movement's basic position that welfare mothers were discouraged from participating in the American political system and discriminated against in other situations as well. The difference between this more conservative and the later more radical groups lay not so much in their core beliefs, as in the actions they recommended to remedy their complaints. Thus many of the more sophisticated AFDC League leaders pointed out that through their participation in the group they had learned how to manipulate the welfare system to their own advantage--to find financial aid for continued education or to acquire part-time employment, particularly with city or social work agencies. Their individual ability in this regard led many AFDC League members to suggest that there obviously were adequate opportunities for individual advancement in American society. As one woman stated: "I don't think welfare people have it so bad right now to tell you the truth. I'm at college. That says something right there."

NWRO ideology discouraged the idea of individual self-help, however, and asserted that the cause of public dependency was to be found in the established order. American social institutions systematically denied to the poor, rights and opportunities which were extended to other citizens as a matter of course. One MWRO leader described the situation in this way:

> Are all people on welfare dishonest or no good?
> It's just that when a mother lives in the sub-
> urbs and has two children, that's just ideal.
> But when you're on welfare and got two children
> you're supposed to be out working and farm those
> kids out. It isn't wonderful any more. Now
> who's made the change here? The system. It's
> saying this mother is wonderful--but if you're
> on welfare you're trash.

NWRO's vision of a better world was one in which the life chances of all recipients could be improved. Believing that individual women's manipulation of the welfare system could not lead to lasting change, NWRO strategists formulated a group strategy which focused on the problems and needs of welfare recipients as a category. In order to achieve the organization's goal of "Bread and Justice," NWRO and its state affiliates planned to overburden the present, and from their point of view, repressive welfare system as the only way of achieving sweeping reforms in governmental programs for the poor. In tactical terms, this position required an organizing strategy which insisted that a recipient become a dues-paying member of her local group before her grievances would be attended to. A great deal of energy was expended within WRO groups in creating the feeling that the welfare of each depended on the welfare of all, and in encouraging the women to act altruistically rather than simply for their own self-interest. For example, staff members put a great deal of pressure on the women to reach the agreement, in advance of a demonstration or large-scale grievance meeting, that no one would leave until everyone's problem had been solved (Piven & Cloward, 1977:279-9).

Although the organizers and the more committed and active welfare mothers were deeply committed to social change and radical welfare reform, they were well aware that the average participant in an MWRO campaign was not so inclined. As a result, the organizers consciously attempted to balance radical action with social activities to keep recipients interested in the organization in between campaigns so "the group wouldn't get the reputation of being all work and no play." Equally as important to these committed leaders as the ultimate goal of social change, however, was their desire to be treated as respectable women in the everyday kind of situation they were most likely to encounter. In addition, the mothers wished to gain access to the knowledge they needed to fight the welfare system at the level of their daily contacts with their caseworker (i.e., a welfare <u>Manual</u>), and to acquire some of the material benefits of an affluent American society. Most important were those goods which have become symbols of status: a decent home, nice furniture, and new clothing.

Old and New Identities

The second generic characteristic of movement ideologies reshapes the participant's self-image and encourages individual and group persistence in sacrifice to the cause and to the special goals of her local group.

By coming to identify with the larger group, movement participants gain a sense of pride and power, and begin to think of themselves as members of an important and potentially influential minority (Gerlach & Hine, 1970:164; 1973:175-6).

Most members of the AFDC League identified with mainstream definitions of the proper female role. This self-image was related to their vision of the future and their hope for social advancement. In order to change the public stereotype of the welfare mother and in order to demonstrate that they were responsible women of good character (i.e., no different from other American women), AFDC League members confined the organization to conventional activities such as giving speaking engagements, giving sedate presentations at the state legislature, continuing their education, and involving themselves in traditional women's organizations like the PTA.

WRO ideology, on the other hand, tried to develop a new identity among welfare mothers by emphasizing the unique, shared experience of their dependence on welfare (Steiner, 1971:288). This new identity had a similar function in the Welfare Mothers Movement as the "black pride" theme had in the earlier Black Power Movement. For the first time, welfare mothers began openly and proudly to identify themselves as recipients:

> To demand recognition and respect for themselves in their present state [without having to meet] existing social requirements for recognition or respect [and to] demand power to control or to share in the control of institutions, even as they reject socially prescribed methods of gaining such power. (Gerlach & Hine, 1970:156)

One MWRO mother put this statement in her own words when she said:

> This is an organization that is trying to give people a stake in how their lives are run and to give them pride in themselves--that they're important. Just because they happen to be on the lower rungs of the economic ladder, they're not worthless. They're human beings no matter what!

This new identity was expressed by a cluster of terms which participants and sympathetic associates of MWRO most frequently used to describe the welfare recipients. The set of terms were: "mothers" and/or "ladies," "citizens," and less frequently "recipients" (in opposition to the welfare system's definition of their identity as "clients"). These terms may seem unimportant to outsiders, but they were extremely salient to MWRO participants. They were the "central symbols" of MWRO's segment of the Welfare Mothers Movement; they defined large areas of related meaning and carried great semantic and evaluative loads for the women (Nicholas, 1973:75).

The first two terms, "mothers" and "ladies," connote two primary aspects of our ideal cultural definition of the female gender role: (1) full-time bearing and raising of children (Bernard, 1979:125); and (2) refined behavior, domestic preoccupation, and dependent, noncompetitive behavior of women who need not work outside the home (Martin & Voorhies, 1975:388-9). Why welfare mothers should select these particular terms is crucial to understanding MWRO's ideology, particularly because such roles have been eschewed by the Women's Liberation Movement (e.g., Adams & Ware, 1979) and because they conflict with the welfare mothers' alternate identity as "citizens." The women's use of the term "citizen," specifically "first-class citizen," was a way of publicly stating that the welfare mothers should be regarded as people entitled to the full privileges and enfranchisements of their nation. This identity was in harmony with the WRO strategy of defining the receipt of welfare as a "right" guaranteed by the laws enacted by Congress rather than a "charity," and carried the inference that participation in the political process was a necessary and proper course of action for these women. Interestingly enough, the rational given by the welfare mothers for much of their political activity, such as testifying before the legislature, was not based on this identity. Whereas this participation in politics should logically have resulted from their status as citizens, in fact most of the women suggested that legislators should pay special attention to their statements, for as mothers, they had the best interests of their children at heart. Why did they more frequently refer to themselves as mothers and ladies than as citizens?

Four factors appear to be involved. First, as a number of scholars have pointed out (Garretson, 1976;
McCourt, 1977; Schneider & Smith, 1973), the dichoto-
my between the female world of home and the male
world of work and politics is more pronounced in the
statements of the lower classes (both white and black,
as Stone, 1979 indicates) than in the upper or middle
classes. According to McCourt, there seems to be a
tendency for the working class women who are most
active in assertive local community organizations to
give even stronger verbal support than other working
class women to traditional familial and sex roles.
For example, they do not agree that wives should have
as much say as their husbands in making important
family decisions. Yet these very active women also
strongly endorse nontraditional extra-familial roles
for women, particularly when these are focused on
problems within their local communities. McCourt
(1977:157) concludes:

> Although the active women do not in any way
> connect their community activities to the wider
> social movement for women's liberation, they are
> obviously acting in ways which are precisely
> those advocated by the ideology of the movement:
> exercising options to get involved in activities
> outside the family and entering arenas of power
> previously reserved for men. And they are ex-
> periencing the effects which the ideology of
> the movement could have predicted. They feel
> a greater sense of personal competence and
> stronger self-esteem, but, in the process, they
> are beginning to experience some conflict about
> their role commitments.

In other words, a second factor underlying the seemingly contradictory identities of mother/lady and
citizen is ambivalence. Women who have not experienced a tradition in which women's loyalties may be
extended beyond the home without fear of personal
and family disruption attempt to resolve their psychological discomfort by strong verbal support of conventional sex roles and identities. This support
convinces themselves and others that, despite the
large portion of their time and energy which go to
outside activities, their major commitment is to their
home and family; they are not neglecting their domestic responsibilities (McCourt, 1977:149, 152).

The third factor which led to an emphasis on MWRO member's identity as mothers and ladies stems from the despised qualities Americans attribute to welfare mothers as a category. Popularly suspected of laziness, promiscuity, illegitimacy and other characteristics with largely negative connotations, these women sought to convey their commitment to mainstream values through their designation as ladies. The frequent use of these terms by the women (and especially by the men associated with MWRO) suggests that conveying a sense of respectability was more crucial to the achievement of group goals than was a concern with sexist language. Furthermore, it would appear especially difficult for women who have been denied an opportunity to act out the idealized female roles in our society, not through their own choice, but because of divorce, desertion or poverty, to move beyond conventional gender attitudes and roles.

Finally, the women's use of the term, mother, made good organizing sense. They were also all "recipients," but there are many categories of recipients in our public welfare system: the aged, the disabled, etc. While these people were not excluded from participating in MWRO, in actuality, they rarely if ever joined. Thus the one common bond which could unite the women on AFDC in an emotional and highly effective way was their motherhood. Even the concept of "sisterhood" prevalent in the Civil Rights Movement and the Women's Liberation Movement could not have been as powerful an identity for these welfare mothers. Indeed, the ideology of the Women's Liberation Movement, especially at that time, denigrated the role of mothers rather than glorifying it.

MWRO members were not averse to referring to themselves as recipients, however, and greatly preferred this term to the more common term, client. MWRO members particularly resented the use of this latter term because it was largely employed by welfare administrators and caseworkers in contexts where the ability of welfare mothers to manage their own affairs was being disputed. Thus for the women, being a client implied discrimination, paternalism and social/political subordination to representatives of the welfare system. Paradoxically, the sense of solidarity generated by MWRO members' use of the term, recipient, could be seen as a valuable corrective to the

implications of their identity as citizens. As
Garretson (1976b:199-200) points out, "the substitu-
tion of an ideal of group welfare for that of individual success constitutes an important innovation
in American social thinking" which began with the
Civil Rights Movement and has been embraced by a wide
variety of minorites and other groups in the United
States in the last decade. She contends, however,
that movements which demand their rights on the
basis of an identity as a citizen actually run counter to this current trend toward emphasizing group
identities as the basis of effective interest groups.
The concept of citizen implies that people must com-
pete as individuals rather than as a group, and
stands in opposition to our use of "protective discrimination" or racial (ethnic, sexual, etc.) quotas
designed to reverse the effects of past inequities.
Thus by emphasizing their identity as recipients,
MWRO members were able to ask for special treatment
by the welfare department on many occasions. The
women argued that not only did the welfare department
have a distinct moral responsibility for its recipients, but also as a public agency was obligated to
listen to and try to accommodate the demands of its
constituents, in this case welfare mothers. Some
MWRO leaders went even further, likening the welfare
department's special relationship with recipients to
that of Americans Indians with the Bureau of Indian
Affairs.

Analysis of the public statements and actions of MWRO
members suggests that the use of these seemingly contradictory identities did not occur randomly, but
with an eye toward maximizing gains and minimizing
losses for the organization. For example, since both
the women's identity as citizens and recipients were
legitimate, the use of them together provided MWRO
members with more leeway in their interactions with
welfare department officials than either one alone.
Welfare administrators could not easily ignore demands
based on the women's legal rights as citizens, nor
could the system turn its back on its clients (Hertz,
1977:606).

If members of the welfare department or other outsiders tried this same tactic of treating MWRO members as if they were no different from other citizens,
however, their attempts were rejected. For example,

the state Department of Public Welfare proposed in 1971 that a flat grant system be instituted in Minnesota in compliance with a federal directive that grant levels be uniform throughout the state. Such a plan would have necessitated abolishing the supplement program which provided funds to replace lost, stolen, or damaged goods. The Commissioner of the DPW tried to justify this plan on the grounds that it placed the recipient in the same situation as other low-income people ("just as WRO always wanted"), who must plan for unexpected major expenditures. In response, MWRO spokeswomen pointed out that recipients are not like the working poor in the open marketplace because they rarely can get credit, loans, or save money from their welfare checks.

Although this response seemed to contradict MWRO's emphasis upon their status as citizens, examination of the women's statements shows that their position was based on a distinction between economic aid and economic control. MWRO participants wished to retain their special economic status with the welfare department when it shielded them from some of the financial shocks experienced by the low-income person. Yet they also demanded that welfare mothers be given as much freedom from oversight and interference in their economic affairs as was possible.

Revolutionary Judo

According to Gerlach and Hine (1973:175-8), the "rule-shifting" evident in the above example is an important feature of all movement ideologies. Such reinterpretation of the rules may allow movement participants to judge the legality of their actions using criteria different from those accepted by the larger society, but is also involved when there is no question about the legality of movement activities (such as when someone simply refuses to play expected subordinate roles or to go through "proper channels"). Similarly, movement participants reinterpret failures or set-backs by emphasizing the minor successes of their actions and view continued opposition as a way of increasing commitment to the cause. Gerlach and Hine call these tactics "revolutionary judo"--techniques which keep the authorities constantly off balance, occasionally by calculated effort but more

often as a result of the very nature of movement ideology. Revolutionary judo involves: (1) exploiting
the gap found in all societies between the ideal for
human (or institutional) behavior and the reality of
actual behavior; (2) shifting the rules on which interaction takes place; and (3) forcing the opposition
to over-react.

Constant emphasis on this ideal-real gap will not
affect those completely opposed to movement goals,
but will very likely increase the previously toler-
able guilt level among more sensitive or vulnerable
members of a society. Minter (1970) suggested that
this was precisely the situation in which the welfare
system found itself in the late 1960s. Under the
influence of the various human rights movements
sweeping the country and the Great Society programs
initiated by the Johnson administration, the welfare
system was particularly vulnerable to the charge that
it was not fulfilling its role of service to the
client. In a speech before the Minnesota Welfare
Association conference, Minter described the situation confronting public agencies in this way:

> [A movement] has to find something that a lot
> of people are going to be for and that [few
> people] are going to be against. Now let's
> take WRO--what are their stated goals and ob-
> jectives? Guaranteed annual income, justice,
> dignity, and democracy. Now who could be
> against those? How can we, as executives of
> agencies, stand up against an organization in
> all out battle who says they're working hard for
> justice, dignity, democracy, and adequate income--
> because that's what we're supposed to be work-
> ing for.

The desire of AFDC League participants to change the
negative image of the welfare mother and their focus
on legislative change predisposed the women to "beating the establishment at its own game," as one leader
described it. Even MWRO chose to lobby rather
than engage in militant demonstrations at the legislature. It is likely then, that the legislative
branch of the government appeared less vulnerable to
tactics of revolutionary judo due to the legitimacy
and authority it was granted as a body of duly elected
representatives of the people. In addition,

112

the AFDC League's method of holding discussions about welfare problems at small private meetings with welfare officials and traditional lobbying held few surprises for the opposition. The only major shift in rules discernible in AFDC League actions was, in fact, that these activities were being carried out for the first time by a nontraditional category of people—poor women. MWRO ideology, on the other hand, urged confrontation as the only effective means of achieving the organization's goals. In order to keep the welfare department and other institutions such as the local school board off balance, MWRO leaders consistently relied on four tactics.

First, the element of surprise was believed to be extremely important. (This was the key reason for MWRO's objections to AFDC League members also participating in MWRO groups.) MWRO strategists believed they must be in a position to present their own version of the problem and their proposed solutions while the opposition was still groping for a response, if the organization was to have any chance for success. By doing research in advance on the issue MWRO wished to raise, the welfare mothers hoped to give the impression that officials risked public exposure if they tried to lie to MWRO members about their intentions or past actions. A second element in MWRO strategy involved an attempt to monopolize the means of communication at a meeting or demonstration by physically controlling the microphone or podium, or by shouting down the opposition. Press releases which clearly set forth the MWRO position were always available, since MWRO leaders believed that good press coverage ensured that the opposition could not simply ignore MWRO or treat the matter as a purely internal issue. Third, MWRO leaders tried to intimidate members of opposing groups by maintaining a strong physical presence in a room—occupying seats near the speaker's platform or near exits in order to convey the impression that a sit-in might occur if their demands were not met. Finally, the women also broke minor rules of decorum. In particular, they realized that their most effective weapon in this respect was to discomfit officials (almost invariably males) by bringing children to what was normatively defined as the male world of public meetings and administrative offices.

Dogmatism

A final characteristic of movement ideologies, whatever the type of movement, has often been called dogmatism or intolerance--the "if-you're-not-for-me-you-
must-be-against-me" philosophy (Gerlach & Hine, 1973:
179). A number of welfare mothers, particularly MWRO
members, suggested that they had become less tolerant
of opposing beliefs as a result of their participation in a movement group. For example, a woman said:

> My husband says I'm very militant now, hard to
> get along with and critical of everything that
> goes on. I know a lot more things than I used
> to, you know. People outside or on TV say,
> "This is happening; this is the way it's sup-
> posed to be." I'll sit there and say, "That's
> a goddamn lie."

Another black woman involved in MWRO described a
conflict with her caseworker in which she refused to
accept behavior which before she would have ignored:

> A couple of weeks ago we went down to the wel-
> fare department because I wanted some money for
> a new bed [which I had asked for earlier]. I
> knew the money could be given me on an emergen-
> cy basis and we went through a hassle about
> that. My eligibility technician finally threw
> a big pile of papers at me and said I would
> have to sign that. I told her I didn't like
> her attitude and asked to see her supervisor.
> I can't imagine myself doing that two years ago.

Finally, the point that the ideology of the Welfare
Mothers Movement cannot be viewed simply as a static,
predictable, and limited set of slogans has been al-
luded to a number of times. An extended example tak-
en from a meeting between John Frederick, the director of the Hennepin County Welfare Department and a
small group of MWRO members will help illustrate,
therefore, the interplay which typically took place
among many of the themes outlined above. (Key
arguments are indicated in the text by underlining.)

The meeting concerned two letters sent by the caseworker of one of MWRO's leaders, Bobby Easton. Present at the meeting were the caseworker, John

Frederick, Leslie Bernstein, Catherine Wood, Rita
Jarvis, Elizabeth James, and six other MWRO members
who took only a small part in the discussion. After
some small talk, the meeting began:

Bobby: At the time I received this letter [from her
    caseworker], I was on my way out of town. The
    whole group of MWRO members was concerned be-
    cause they were wondering if this would affect
    them--if the other workers would feel the same
    way toward them as my worker felt toward me.
    This is the letter here. I had just got burned
    out of my house a couple of weeks before. This
    letter says: "I was just contacted by [your old
    landlord] for nonpayment of rent for 17 days
    in February for $39.00. It would be wise to
    see that this amount is paid immediately to a-
    void indignation (sic) proceedings of the court.
    I would also like to take this time to arrange
    an appointment with you for Thursday afternoon
    to make a home visit. Perhaps we can just
    talk about your views and evaluations of the
    various roles you are involved in. For instance
    those of the community leader because of your
    Welfare Rights involvement and those of a mother
    and homemaker that your children demand of you.
    How do these roles materially interaffect one
    another and how and why do you assign priorities
    to your obligations? These are just a few of
    the subjects you ought to think on." [I didn't
    have the meeting though, because] I had to leave
    town that day for a Welfare Rights meeting.

Frederick: So your concern in meeting with me was to
    discuss the things stated in your letter?

Bobby: Like the question to me, when I got the let-
    ter, was almost like a threat that maybe I was
    not taking care of my children as well as I
    should, and maybe my role in the organization
    is taking me away from them and I should get
    out of it. In between the lines, you know.

Frederick: But you don't really know this. It might
    have been what it implied, but you don't know
    because you did not have the meeting. As I see
    it, the role between social worker and client
    is one of confidentiality, closeness, and inti-
    macy. I would expect that there would be a lot

115

of items that would be discussed of this type.

Rita: Why is it that the welfare worker is concerned with how much time she's spending with Welfare Rights? Welfare Rights is trying to protect her children. . . Why does the worker have to know this and why does she have to come out and question her about what her priorities are? She's a mother. Where does she think her priorities belong?

Frederick: Well, let me ask you something Rita. I have a child every day who is battered. I'm not saying that everyone in the Rights Organization batters. . . but we have a legal right to go in and see the child is being cared for.

Caseworker: I offered her services--to come out and let her explain to me how she felt about her work and her children and whether there were any problems I might help her with. I feel that anyone who leaves the home, even social workers with families, have a lot to think about. I'm sorry she misunderstood.

Frederick: I see nothing wrong here, overt or covert, that implies in any way that a representative of this department attempted to undermine the role you want to play. We are trying to meet need, but we are also trying to be responsible and make sure that we meet the need of those with the greatest need. We have on our rolls, I suspect, people that are not eligible, and we're trying to even give service to them.

Leslie: I think there is a much larger issue here. Why, because a woman is on welfare, does another member of society have a right to question their performance as a mother and their activities? To me, it seems that, if you're on welfare, that makes you a second-class citizen. She [the social worker] said, "even social workers have problems with children when they work," but who calls them up? . . . . I feel that unless there is evidence that Bobby's children are neglected --they've got bruises--I don't think that a recipient (and I call this being harassed) should have her ability as a mother questioned.

Frederick: I'm going to take a very hard stand on this. Bobby turned to you [and you thought],

116

"What can we make of this and go down and
present this to the director." I refuse to
make anything of this.

Betty Ann: I'm taking courses at the university and
I think this letter is a real intimidation.

Leslie: The problem is that recipients don't get
enough money and the letter didn't ask Bobby
if she wanted social services.

Caseworker: I "offered" them to her.

Leslie: If she wants them, she can ask for them
like any other citizen.

Elizabeth: That letter is so impersonal. She is educated and has forgotten the idea that the welfare mother is not aware of what goes on here as
an establishment. You're not a recipient, but
you know how it is being black [speaking to the
caseworker]. When someone comes up to you and
says, "You're black," right away you get defen-
sive. The way this letter is written, a welfare
recipient says, "that's an attack." If she
had said she would like to get to know Bobby
better and said nothing about her children.

Leslie: What are you trying to do? Get rid of the
leaders?

Frederick: The dialogue has been broken, but let's
try to keep it open in the future. There are
more important issues we can work on together.

Elizabeth: I assume that the worker was mainly concerned about the children since Bobby was
taking welfare money, but she should also be
treated with dignity and respect.

Catherine: Let's just say it was a misunderstanding.

In this excerpt from the meeting, each side attempted
to have its definition of the problem accepted as
correct. On Leslie's suggestion, MWRO tried to gain
the upper hand by setting up a meeting ostensibly
with only a few mothers, but then changing the "rules"
by bringing top leaders from all the locals to argue
Bobby's case. Frederick quickly tried to dismiss
MWRO's complaint altogether by pointing out that since
no meeting had taken place, the worker's intentions
could not have been known. He constantly emphasized

that he wished to dialogue with MWRO and pointed out
that he had cooperated with them in the past. He
described himself as "responsible," and implied
that the mothers were intemperate. He managed to
divert some of the meeting to a discussion of social
worker/client relations and suggested that women who
get welfare sometimes treat their children badly
(i.e., batter them), hinting that such children can
be removed from undesirable homes.

MWRO members did not appear to be aware of the sexist
and paternalistic tone of many of Frederick's re-
marks (Johnson and Holton, 1976, have recently pointed out this kind of bias was built into the administration of AFDC assistance). Instead, the MWRO leaders
based their arguments on their identities as mothers,
while Leslie emphasized that of citizen. After the
welfare mothers were unsuccessful in getting Frederick
to censure the caseworker on those bases, however,
one of MWRO's leaders began to use MWRO's alternate
identity as recipient by portraying the women as un-
educated, at a disadvantage vis-a-vis the welfare
department, and deserving of special consideration.
Finally, although they did not really believe it,
several MWRO leaders agreed to write off the episode
as a case of misunderstanding in order to minimize
the impact of their failure. The statements of MWRO
participants in this meeting also expressed the
three core beliefs outlined for the movement as a
whole--the right to self-determination, to human
dignity, and the need to organize in order to achieve
their goals.

Many of the outsiders who had contact with movement
groups were genuinely perplexed by the ambiguity, rule-
shifting, and identities which the welfare mothers
used. As Gerlach and Hine (1973:179) point out, "many
people admire commitment while decrying a dogmatic
ideological stance." The two go hand in hand, however,
for the risk-taking and commitment required of participants demand the conviction that one's beliefs are
worth the sacrifice. In this way the dogmatism of
movement ideology is closely related to two other
factors crucial to the spread of a movement--total
personal commitment and the recruitment of new members
into movement groups. It is to these two factors
that we will now turn.

CHAPTER 6

Recruitment and Commitment

It is tempting for observers to attribute recruitment
and commitment to a movement to the emotional impact
and drama (or "mass hysteria") of rallies and demonstrations, to the charisma of a well-known leader, or
to the appeal of the ideology (or theology) of a movement. After years of collecting information on
active participants in a variety of movements, however, Gerlach and Hine (1970:87, 94-5) suggest these
events may facilitate a conversion experience, but
rarely initially bring an individual into the organization of the movement.

Recruitment

For one thing, people do not join an amorphous movement per se, but are recruited through face-to-face
contact with a committed member of a specific group
within the total movement network. Gerlach and Hine
(1970:79) suggest that:

> No matter how a typical participant describes
> his reasons for joining the movement, or what
> motives may be suggested by a social scientist
> on the basis of deprivation, disorganization,
> or deviance models, it is clear that the origi-
> nal decision to join required some contact with
> the movement. This is such an obvious fact that
> it is generally overlooked in analyses of move-
> ments. . . . We found few cases, either among
> our questionnaire respondents or in our case
> histories, in which the original contact was not
> a personal one. This contact almost always in-
> volved a significant, pre-existing relationship
> --a relative, a close friend, a neighbor, an
> influential associate of some sort--with whom the
> new convert had had a meaningful interaction
> prior to recruitment.

Actual recruitment to a movement is thus the result
of the willingness of individual members to persuade
others they already know to accept new beliefs and to
participate in a group. In other words, it is not

disruption that facilitates the spread of a movement, for where social disorganization and community disintegration exist, recruitment to movements actually appears to be least effective (Gerlach & Hine, 1970: 84-6).[1]

Modification of the Gerlach-Hine model. Kaplan (1966) alludes to a similar point in his description of the growth of the AFDC League in Minnesota:

> In almost any community, there are attacks on
> AFDC families, cutbacks in financial assistance
> . . . chronic grievances, and frustrations, real
> or imagined. Any of these can serve as a focal
> point for the organizing of a group. The basic
> ingredient, however, is the willingness of a
> small group of AFDC mothers to start an organi-
> zation.

Analyses of the case histories of the founders of several Welfare Mothers Movement groups in the state does indeed show that initially small groups of two to three women who already knew each other decided to organize a welfare mothers' group. The majority of the early membership of the AFDC League and MWRO, however, were not recruited through significant preexisting relationships, as the Gerlach-Hine model hypothesizes. Rather, the most common pattern which emerged was for this small core of women to turn immediately to relatively impersonal means of recruitment to build the membership of the organization. For example, the women would cultivate (hopefully favorable) publicity in the local news media or canvass low-income areas informing everyone in the neighborhood that a new welfare mothers group had been organized. Some recruitment did take place through the personal relationships of committed members and the staff of these movement groups, but this remained a much less common alternate pattern.

This reliance by movement groups in Minnesota on impersonal recruitment techniques was the result of: (1) constraints on the behavior of women in our society; (2) the special characteristics of welfare mothers; (3) features of the movement's urban setting; and (4) changes in the political climate. A more complete description of the ways in which welfare mothers were brought into movement groups will enable us to examine the impact of each of these factors on the special recruiting problems of welfare mothers.

Recruiting welfare recipients. Initially the idea of forming an AFDC League arose among a small group of women involved in the YWCA Solo Parents group in St. Paul, Minnesota in 1966. Two women in particular took the initiative in forming an organization. They announced the formation of this new group, as well as the date and site selected for its first meeting, in the local radio and newspapers. Fliers, notices of meetings, and later the group's newsletter, were posted in both public and private welfare agencies and food stamp centers in the major urban areas of the state. The AFDC League gained between 80 and 100 members largely as a result of this initial publicity campaign. AFDC League leaders continued to rely on these techniques throughout the group's existence and believed them to be very effective. Most of the core of committed, long-term members stated, in fact, that they knew no one in the organization before they joined, yet had decided to attend their first meeting of an AFDC League satellite group due to this kind of publicity. After the AFDC League had been in operation for several months, some recruitment through personal relationships more closely approximating the pattern suggested by the Gerlach-Hine model began to take place. For example, the development of friendly contacts between the staff of local community groups and AFDC League leaders or staff, such as June Waldheim, occasionally led to the recruitment of individual women or the affiliation of an entire group with the AFDC League. Some individual welfare mothers active in the group also reported recruiting a neighbor or friend, rarely a relative, into their group.

The recruitment techniques used to form Direct Action Recipients of Welfare in 1968, however, matches precisely the pattern suggested by Gerlach and Hine. This was the only group to use pre-existing personal relationships almost exclusively as a means of recruiting members. As a group, Direct Action differed in a number of ways from the rest of the Welfare Mothers Movement groups in Minnesota. It was the smallest and shortest-lived group, having at its height only about 25 members and lasting about a year before splitting into two factions, one of which began to recruit for MWRO. This lack of interest in developing a mass base for the group and the previous associational experience of its early members appear to be the crucial explanatory differences. Direct Action members, although they were largely welfare mothers, knew each other through their involvement in activist community organizations which had focused largely on nonwelfare issues. Thus when it was first formed, Direct Action was composed of women who saw themselves as a part of the larger radical left movement, rather than primarily as members of a welfare mothers group. Direct Action did focus exclusively on welfare issues, however, and for this reason soon attracted a number of more assertive AFDC League members who wished to participate in the activities of both groups. The contacts which had led to the formation of Direct Action, however, were based on the women's interest in nonwelfare issues. This focus obviated the major recruiting difficulty experienced by other movement groups--the stigma of welfare and the consequent unwillingness of most recipients to identify themselves as welfare mothers and become publicly involved in a movement group.[2]

MWRO, however, was committed to developing a mass-based organization and so chose to recruit primarily through what were called "door-knocking campaigns." The small core of interested members from Direct Action, along with an NWRO organizer and a few VISTAs, formed the recruiting nucleus. Working in groups of twos (ideally a racially mixed group including one welfare mother and a staff person), they canvassed low-income neighborhoods, distributing literature and talking about the way in which WROs tried to increase benefits to those on welfare. Any indication of interest in MWRO led to a follow-up visit by other welfare mothers and staff, who told the woman more about WRO and urged her to attend a meeting planned in her neighborhood. The closest approximation to a "pre-existing significant relationship" in these recruiting drives was an occasional attempt to include someone with a respected position in the neighborhood, such as a local minister, on the door-knocking team. Door-knocking did involve face-to-face contact, but since women living in a neighborhood knew personally only a small fraction of the residents, their inclusion on the recruiting team could hardly be interpreted as supporting the Gerlach-Hine hypothesis.

Door-knocking campaigns did result in the mobilization of hundreds of welfare mothers for MWRO's clothing, furniture, and Title I campaigns. These recipients were exposed to the ideology and goals of MWRO, but were primarily interested in getting more benefits for themselves from the welfare department, rather than in long-term membership in the organization. One leader of MWRO described most participants' motives in this way:

> Fight the system? No, people who join Welfare Rights don't know anything about it except Adequate Income, Dignity, and Justice. When they join Welfare Rights it's for a campaign, and when you door-knock them, you tell them that what we are asking for is a right. That way when they come into Welfare Rights they don't feel they're getting all they're supposed to be getting from the welfare department.

As was true with the AFDC League, however, important personal relationships did serve as links through which a small number of welfare mothers were recruited to MWRO locals, particularly after the organization had been in existence for several months. Most MWRO leaders reported they had spoken to some of their friends and neighbors about the organization and occasionally had even convinced someone to join. These leaders were perplexed, however, because most of the women they brought in in this way did little more than attend a single meeting or participate in one campaign. Staff members and nonrecipients associated with MWRO, such as Carl Jones and Sam Putnam, also told women about MWRO and urged them to join if they were having welfare problems--although this was never a major source of new members. In addition, one MWRO leader told me that she was asked by the MWRO organizer to be part of a door-knocking team for a section of the city where she had once lived. Despite her earlier residence there, however, most of the new members who joined from that area were not her previous neighbors or acquaintances, but were strangers.

Factors affecting recruitment. The difficulty which

movement groups faced in recruiting welfare mothers
into newly formed organizations (with the exception
of Direct Action) stemmed from a number of related
factors. These factors include the constraints of
their sex and poverty, cultural differences, and
special characteristics of the urban and political
environment. These variables worked together to reinforce the isolation and lack of solidarity found
among welfare mothers as a category. Leslie Bernstein
touched on many of these factors during an interview
about her recruiting experiences in both Massachusetts
and in Minnesota:

> There was one group [in Boston] that was in a
> housing project that was really weak and one
> there that was really strong, but then died out.
> I think a lot more depended on the nature of
> the people more than whether the group was lo-
> cated in [a housing] project or not. It seemed
> that certain areas of Boston were fairly con-
> servative and others weren't--were fairly
> militant. We always went better in the more mil-
> itant. There was this whole black thing about
> how they had been put down and stuff. There
> were a lot of poor Irish and Italian, however,
> who because of their culture (women were in the
> background) looked down on demonstrating. . . .
> I don't feel there's any sense of community in
> the Southside [of Minneapolis] although Model
> Cities pretends there is. Maybe part of it is
> that the Southside group members are all spread
> out. But on the Northside there is an identi-
> fiable community feeling. Yes, I think that's
> the basic factor. If it's not a black thing,
> that kind of a community ("we're all persecuted
> blacks"), then it's got to be some other kind of
> thing. There hasn't been a whole lot of success
> with Welfare Rights being that kind of link.
> There's usually some kind of link there already.

The Welfare Mothers Movement differs from the other
movements studied by Gerlach and Hine and on which
they base their model because its members were drawn
almost exclusively from a single sex (even after NWRO
attempted to broaden membership eligibility to include
the working poor). Clearly our cultural assumptions
about the appropriate roles and spheres of activity
for women must play an important part in the recruit-

ing difficulties experienced by Welfare Mothers
Movement groups. As Freeman (1979:561) suggests:

> It has long been known that people can be kept
> down as long as they are kept divided from each
> other, relating more to their social superiors
> than to their social equals. . . [For example,]
> women have generally been deprived of struc-
> tured interaction and been kept isolated in
> their individual homes, relating more to men
> than to each other.

Hacker (1979:508-9) amplifies on this observation by
pointing out that women in our culture have difficulty
developing a feeling of group identification and
have less freedom of movement than their male counter-
parts. These constraints on the activities of mainstream American women are accentuated in other cultural or subcultural groups. Women in many minorities are frequently socialized almost exclusively
within their own group and may be discouraged from
even forming ties with women from other ethnic or
racial categories.

In Minnesota, although there were no prominent white
ethnic groups (other than the large number of
Minnesotans of Scandinavian descent) and relatively
little racial segregation, the American Indian population does provide a good example of Hacker's obser-
vations. None of the Welfare Mothers Movement groups
were very successful in recruiting among the Indian
population, although the AFDC League had a small
group of Indian women who formed their own separate
satellite group in Minneapolis. MWRO also attempted
to door-knock in an area on the southside of
Minneapolis where Indians tended to be concentrated.
By the late 1960s, however, the Indian community had
developed its own movement. As one of the MWRO members involved in the recruiting effort pointed out:

> We didn't get a large reception because AIM [the
> American Indian Movement] got the people under
> control. When they can go to AIM for everything
> --for all their problems--why should they go to
> another outside organization, even if we have
> the same goals as AIM. We would have had to work
> through the AIM office, have AIM refer them to
> us or something.

Not only did Indians have their own racial/ethnic organization then, but there is also evidence that many groups of urban Indians prefer to use their own tribal "survival networks" or to retreat to the reservation and the BIA in times of extreme financial need rather than deal with outsiders or urban institutions (Guillemin, 1975:249).

Thus there are constraints which effectively discourage all women in our society from engaging in public political activities and additional restrictions on welfare mothers as a category. First, welfare budgets are rarely generous enough to include the money for daycare or nonmedical travel which is necessary for participation in community organizations. Second, welfare recipients are a special subset of our population with even fewer bases for solidarity than the average American woman. They are set apart from middle- and upper-class women, who often have negative or at best ambivalent attitudes towards welfare mothers, and divided among themselves by racial or ethnic antagonisms and by their own acceptance of the stigma society attaches to their status as public dependents. Even the women involved in the movement were torn between personal negative feelings about other welfare mothers and the positive view of recipients demanded by movement ideology. For example, many of my informants suggested that before they joined a movement group, they felt that they were different from those "other" recipients who were probably (as popular stereotypes suggested) lazy, immoral, and shiftless. In some cases this attitude persisted even after the women became committed to the movement, for the women reasoned that those welfare mothers who really wanted to better their lives would have become involved in a movement group. As one MWRO leader stated:

> Actually, you know it's just money in the bank is where the difference is between us and other people. Lots of the Welfare Rights people is smart ladies. If they'd been totally poor thinking, they wouldn't be out fighting to better their conditions while on ADC [AFDC] and change policies. . . or to get to a level where they could get off welfare.

Of course, not all welfare mothers in the United

States exist outside a close-knit network or community of friends and relatives. Stack (1974:102-3), for example, found that domestic networks composed of kin and close friends who exchange goods and services in times of need were prevalent among the poor blacks she studied in a Midwestern city. In that population, a high percentage of a woman's kin were likely to be dependent on welfare at any one point in time. Such a situation very likely might have resulted in recruitment to a movement through kin links, as the Gerlach-Hine model proposes.

The welfare mothers in Minneapolis who became involved in Welfare Mothers Movement groups could not use these kinds of links or networks, however. Very few women brought relatives into their movement group because few of the women's relatives were or ever had been on welfare (other than Old Age Assistance). In addition, about half of the active participants in movement groups in Minneapolis reported that they rarely had contact with their relatives at all because many of them were ashamed to have a family member on welfare. Nor did all those relatives who did maintain contact with a sister or daughter on welfare approve of her involvement in a movement group.[3] Relatives who were not on welfare were explicitly barred from joining MWRO when it was first formed (the AFDC League simply had no policy on the issue), but they could have joined an auxiliary group called the Friends of Welfare Rights which was created specifically for nonrecipient supporters. Only a handful of relatives joined the Friends, however. Others either disapproved of the women's activities with a militant group such as MWRO, did not know of the Friends' existence, or were simply reluctant to pay the $10-15 membership dues per year to an organization which provided no direct benefit for themselves.

The relatively small amount of generational dependency among the welfare mothers involved in movement groups in Minnesota undoubtedly contributed to the women's infrequent use of kin ties for recruitment. On the other hand, two characteristics of the active women in these movement organizations could have facilitated recruitment through pre-existing personal relationships, but obviously did not to any great extent. First, these women were in no sense transients

or new residents in the city or state. Most were
born in Minnesota and had lived in Minneapolis for
at least ten years or longer. Second, the average
length of dependency was greater among movement participants than the state-wide average of the time.
AFDC League informants had a mean length of 6.5 years
and MWRO members 4.2 years on welfare, as compared
to the state average of 3 years (The State of
Minnesota, 1965). It is plausible to hypothesize
that a longer period of dependency or local residence
might have resulted in a wide range of contacts with
other welfare recipients. Since there are few opportunities for structured interaction among welfare
mothers (outside of welfare department waiting rooms),
however, it is extremely unlikely that these characteristics could have produced a large circle of
mutually acquainted recipients who could have recruited one another into movement groups. Longer than
average dependence on welfare may have predisposed
individual welfare mothers to join a movement group
as a means of changing their lives, but did not facilitate recruitment through "pre-existing personal
relationships."

Special features of the urban environment in
Minneapolis also affected the recruiting techniques
used by Welfare Mothers Movement groups. For example, there were no large public housing projects
such as frequently are found in other major cities
in the United States. The projects which did exist
were modest in scale, relatively well-maintained,
and contained many low-income families who were not
on welfare. In other words, a welfare mother could
not assume that a neighbor or acquaintance was on
welfare, and if she did not wish her dependency to
be widely known, was unlikely to discuss welfare
issues with others. This situation was even more
pronounced in other types of neighborhoods, as low-
cost housing tended to be scattered throughout the
city rather than confined to well defined ghettos.
As one black woman in MWRO, who had moved to the city
nine years before from Detroit, said:

> Even if your parents were poor or on welfare,
> just going to school in Minneapolis, being
> bussed around, and knowing better conditions
> than you live under and the way others think
> means that it's hard to "think poor."

Finally, changes in the political arena affected recruitment to the movement. Minnesota, and especially the city of Minneapolis, had a long history of progressive city and state government. The state and county welfare departments in urban areas facilitated the recruitment of members to the AFDC League in particular by allowing the organization to post notices and distribute leaflets in their waiting rooms. On the other hand, the early 1970s saw the emergence of the "silent majority" and attempts to reduce welfare spending in the state. Welfare mothers were well aware of this new mood and many pointed out that the climate of the times made it more difficult to recruit welfare recipients--particularly into groups such as MWRO which advocated militant tactics.

Thus welfare mothers in Minnesota are good examples of what McCarthy and Zald (1977:1228) call "isolated constituents." They suggest that the media in particular mediate the relationship between isolated potential constituents and social movement organizations. The media do this by creating awareness of the existence of the organizations and by convincing potential constituents that movement goals are (or should be) their personal goals as well, thereby predisposing them to join a movement group. McCarthy and Zald also hypothesize that where potential social movement constituents do not normally meet in face-to-face interaction, professional staff must be assigned the task of developing movement cells. The Gerlach-Hine strategy of recruitment through pre-existing significant relationships is feasible among welfare mothers, then, only where there are heavy concentrations of potential movement participants with functioning local groups or personal networks and an identifiable community feeling.

Commitment

Welfare mothers did experience opposition from various segments of the established order throughout the decade in the form of harassment from the general public, fear of reprisals from the welfare department, and even arrests. There is, however, a crucial balance between an optimum level of opposition which serves to enhance and bring about recruitment and commitment to a movement, and strong opposition which destroys groups or intimidates participants (Gerlach & Hine, 1970:186-8). Nevertheless, personal risk-taking and commitment--the fourth key factor in the spread of a movement--go hand in hand. Gerlach and Hine (1970:158) define commitment as:

> A psychosocial state which results from an identity-altering experience and a bridge-burning act. It is manifested as (a) primacy of concern with the belief system of the movement; (b) participation in the social organization of the movement; (c) some degree of charismatic ability to influence others; (d) willingness to risk social, economic, or political sanctions exercised by opponents of the movement; and (e) some degree of behavioral change.

A movement participant is prepared for the commitment experience through a series of steps which may either occur gradually or be compressed in time so that recruitment is followed swiftly by commitment to the movement and its goals. Despite differences in detail, however, the general form of the commitment experience has three major components: (1) one or more subjective, highly emotional experiences leading to significant change in the person's identity; (2) an act, or series of acts which cuts the individual off from conventional society and identifies him or her with the movement; and (3) a social context (almost invariably a small group) which provides for close interaction and group support for changed cognitive and behavioral patterns (Gerlach & Hine, 1973:180-2). A close look at the commitment experiences of members of the AFDC League and MWRO supports Gerlach and Hine's contention that this is a general process characteristic of all social movements.

The AFDC League/A growth in self-confidence. AFDC League informants invariably began a description of the process which led to their decision to become involved in the movement by discussing the feelings they had when they first applied for welfare. At that time, they experienced doubt about their own self-worth and were painfully aware that others no longer viewed them as respectable wives and mothers. One of the major changes which they experienced after joining an AFDC League group, however, was a new awareness that other women were having similar

problems and feelings. Every informant volunteered
an example of an individual who had undergone a major
transformation in her attitudes and behavior as a
result of talking and interacting with other AFDC
League members. These changes involved a growth in
self-confidence, a feeling of greater control over
the course the woman's life was to take, and increased
political and organizational sophistication.

Publicly joining in AFDC League lobbying efforts or
helping another woman with a problem at the welfare
department were not easy acts for most of these
welfare mothers. Despite the fact that many administrators in their county departments verbally supported their efforts to improve the public image of
the welfare recipient and to change state welfare
legislation, most of the women commented that, <u>at
that time</u>, they felt that a great deal of risk was
involved in their activities. In other words, as
Gerlach and Hine (1970:143) point out, "the risk
of commitment is relative to both the individual and
the situation." For middle-class women to protest
welfare policies would entail little risk; for a
welfare mother, identical actions could lead to the
loss of her benefits, the removal of her children
from an unsuitable home, or at the very least, the
kind of public exposure of her dependency which she
previously worked so hard to avoid.

AFDC League members believed these risks stemmed
primarily from their involvement in a political
organization (as opposed to a social or therapeutic
group) "at a time when such actions by welfare
mothers were unheard of." Nevertheless, the respect
and attention eventually given the women by both legislators and administrators during their lobbying
efforts (regardless of whether those efforts were
successful or not) were crucial reactions. For as
Gerlach and Hine (1970:112) indicate, ordinarily
"the bait of demonstrable power is necessary for any
but the most pathological individual to move toward
the risks of full commitment."

In addition, the segmentation of the AFDC League into
small neighborhood satellite groups provided the kind
of mutual support and close interaction with other
committed members which best ensure the survival of
changed thought and behavior patterns. Even those

satellite groups which emphasized political issues
included social activities on their agenda, thus
reinforcing the sense that the women were interested
in each other not simply for instrumental or ideological reasons, but for personal ones as well. Most
AFDC League members formed close friendships with
other women in the group and encouraged each other
to overcome feelings of personal inadequacy. In
some instances this simply made the woman more comfortable with her role as a full-time mother. In
other cases it led to job training or completion of
the woman's education in preparation for re-entering
the job market.

MWRO/Confrontation. The commitment experiences reported by MWRO informants differed in content somewhat from those of AFDC League members, but followed
the same general pattern. The major differences
consisted of the speed of the commitment process and
the context of the bridge-burning act. Little time
elapsed, for example, between the woman's initial
recruitment into MWRO and an emotional event such as
participating in a demonstration or being arrested.
Thus much of the commitment process for these women
took place in a dramatic and highly visible context,
rather than in the less visible setting of small
group meetings or in sedate presentations at sub-
committee hearings in the state capital, as had been
the case for AFDC League members.

Many MWRO leaders reported that they had become committed to the movement during their initial demonstration. There were long periods of time during
the daily sit-ins at the welfare department in which
friendships with other welfare mothers in the group
developed and a deeper awareness of the organization's
long range goals was gained through discussions with
each other and MWRO's organizer, Tina Czernek. Carl
Jones described the process by which normally law-
abiding welfare mothers were prepared to be arrested
for disturbing the peace:

> The militancy grew. Even the first mothers who
> came in were not ready to get arrested. But the
> system works for us. When you go down and ask
> and [the welfare department officials] shilly-
> shally or make a promise and then don't come
> through with it--this makes you madder. This is

where Tina was an expert at interpreting to the
mothers and being a spokesman for them and
attacking the establishment; making the mothers
see themselves as righteous and the establishment
as evil. The militancy grew along with the
sense of being misused and abused. They began
to see it and were willing to do something
about it.

The commitment process was sustained by the continu-
ous efforts of the staff to strengthen these new
attitudes among recruits. As one mother said, "Tina
called the mothers all the time and was close; she
had meetings and never lost contact with us."

Not all welfare mothers who participated in the lobbying efforts of the AFDC League or in MWRO demonstrations became committed to their organization or the
larger Welfare Mothers Movement, however. As Kaplan
(1966) points out, during any one period there is a
high turnover of women getting welfare benefits and
"a mother who views herself as temporarily needing
AFDC is not likely to be recruited to a group or
develop a 'cause' about the program." Indeed, the
great majority of MWRO members were interested only
in obtaining benefits for themselves and had no real
intention of becoming involved in the group on a
continuing basis. As Gerlach and Hine (1973:183-4)
indicate, critics often delight in stories about the
Cadillacs and expensive clothing of movement leaders
or stigmatize all participants as in it to make a fast
buck. Certainly there were welfare mothers who did
not have a clue as to what personal transformation
and social change were all about, but writing off
most participants as self-seeking opportunists is a
mistake which can lead to a serious underestimation
of the impact of a social movement. This attitude,
however, was at the heart of much of the Minnesota
welfare system's early response to MWRO activities,
which were dismissed as the result of "outside agitators" whose "purpose was to destroy the traditional
public welfare system" in the state.

In fact, most of the core members of MWRO wrly pointed out that "MWRO never did anything for me," for
few of these women had received any tangible benefits
through grievance work or as a result of MWRO's campaigns (although other members had). This core of

women continued to participate in the group, however, because they had become convinced that their efforts would eventually change the welfare system and thus indirectly benefit themselves and their families, as well as other welfare mothers. As one woman said:

> I've learned a lot of things that I didn't know about but after you get into any organization that's fighting the system or fighting for a cause you grow up quite a bit in education ways. I mean, I never knew a damn thing about politics. I never knew a damn thing except cleaning house and serving drinks and making love to my husband and taking care of my children. I didn't need to know any more. (Hertz, 1977:610)

In any social movement some groups will emphasize demands for social change, while others will focus primarily on bringing about personal transformation (Gerlach & Hine, 1973:180-2). Those who judge the success of the Welfare Mothers Movement (or any other movement) solely in terms of their stated goals about welfare reform or social change, however, frequently ignore the impact of personal change among participants. Piven and Cloward (1977:352-3), however, do fail to consider this aspect of the commitment process in order to focus exclusively on the public political goals of NWRO, and so are forced to conclude:

> NWRO failed to achieve its own objective--to build an enduring mass organization through which the poor could exert influence. Certainly NWRO did not endure; it survived a mere six or seven years, then collapsed. Just as certainly, it did not attract a mass base. . . . And it is our opinion that it had relatively little influence on the lobbying process to which it progressively devoted most of its resources. But in the final analysis we do not judge NWRO a failure for these reasons. . . . Rather, we judge it by another criterion: whether it exploited the momentary unrest among the poor to obtain the maximum concessions possible in return for the restoration of quiescence. It is by that criterion that it failed.

Gerlach and Hine, on the other hand, argue that personal transformation is a far better gauge of movement strength than the success or failure of a specific demonstration or the ability to force the established order to meet certain demands. Moreover, a prominent focus on personal change in individual lifestyles can be found in a number of contemporary social movements, including the Women's Liberation Movement. For example, Freeman (1979:561-3) suggests that the younger branch of the movement attaches great significance to "rap groups" which bring women together for the first time in a situation where interaction can take place. These groups alter the participants' perceptions of themselves and their society through a process which has come to be called "consciousness-raising." The resocialization of one's self-concept is both irreversible and contagious. Even those who drop out of the movement spread feminist ideas among their friends and colleagues, thus indirectly serving as a mechanism for wider social change as well. Likewise, Gerlach and Hine (1973:183) describe the lasting personal change which has been commented on by many ex-radicals from the early days of the Student Movement. Many had become disillusioned with demonstrations and violent tactics, but either believed they were different people than they would have been had they never become involved in the movement, or were still pursuing personal and social change in other less newsworthy ways.

The impact of personal change is, unfortunately, difficult to assess. There is some indirect evidence, other than the statements of welfare mothers, which does attest to its significance within the Welfare Mothers Movement. For example, on a number of occasions when women had dropped out of either the AFDC League or MWRO, they were still willing to become actively involved again when a crisis arose which required the efforts of large numbers of women. Many continued to witness to others about the positive changes in their lives which resulted from their participation in a movement group. In addition, Piven and Cloward (1977:298-9) themselves have pointed out that the grievance activities of welfare rights organizations created a body of recipients who were experienced in dealing with the welfare system and so "no longer required the aid of the group in solving their individual problems or those of their friends and neighbors. . . a circumstance that continually depleted the ranks of organized groups."

Grievance work by former WRO members may not have coincided with the group-oriented radical political ideology of greatest importance to Piven and Cloward, but does suggest that personal change had taken place among WRO participants, enabling many women to deal more assertively and effectively with their problems. Finally, a study by HEW cited in Piven and Cloward's earlier work (1971:326-7) indicates that, although "the number of AFDC women who reported they belonged to WROs was very small in all cities. . . there was a strong inverse relation between the percentage of WRO members and the number of recipients who felt helpless (the more WRO members in a city, the fewer the number of recipients who felt powerless)."

To underestimate the role of personal transformation through the commitment experience then is to misunderstand a major way in which movements accelerate social change (Gerlach & Hine, 1973:183). Alteration in the lives of welfare mothers participating in a movement group was testimony to others about the potential power of their ideas.

FOOTNOTES

1. As Gerlach and Hine (1970:84) indicate, we must be careful when dealing with unfamiliar communities or subgroups. What appears to be social disorganization simply may be forms of social organization other than those characteristic of middle-class America.

2. This situation is similar to one Freeman (1979:568) describes for the Women's Liberation Movement in which two factions split over whether the movement should be a branch of the radical left or become an independent women's movement, i.e., whether the enemy was "capitalism" or male-dominated social institutions and values.

3. My 34 key informants were all long-term (six months or more) members of their group. Of 15 AFDC League informants, four were black, ten were white, and one an American Indian. Of 19 MWRO members, eight were black and 11 were white. The mean age of the women at the time they joined their group was 34.5 years for AFDC League members and 30.6 years for MWRO informants.

CHAPTER 7

Opposition and Support

As it has been used here, commitment can only be understood in the context of risk, and risk is directly related to the fifth factor of opposition in the Gerlach-
Hine (1973:184) model of movement dynamics. All social
movements inevitably generate opposition from some segment of the larger society and must, in turn, develop
a "we-they" or ingroup-outgroup orientation among movement participants. These outgroups and the impact of
external events, however, have often been ignored in
the anthropological and sociological literature on
the growth and decline of social movements. This
neglect has both a methodological and theoretical basis.

The External Context

Neglect of the external context of social movements
stems in part from an error in one of the first steps
of research design--the selection of the unit of analysis. The social movement, to early observers, seemed
a natural system with obvious boundaries in time and
space--a close analogue to the groups and societies
which were traditionally selected as research units.
Anthropologists in particular excluded consideration
of nonparticipants and external events for fear that
an increase in the scale of the research would inter-
fere with the holistic approach which was an important
aspect of traditional fieldwork methods. In fact,
however, narrowly defining the unit of analysis and
relevant variables actually led to a loss of context,
interrelationship, and process which heretofore had
been the strength of anthropology and ethnography
(Eames & Goode, 1977:262, 273).

When the population selected is poor, this tendency to
focus on communities or organizations as bounded units
and to exclude their institutional environments is reinforced by several contemporary theories of poverty.
As Jones (1972:52-3) points out, the culture of poverty
concept in particular leads the observer to assume a
priori that the poor (usually nonwhite) community is
a relatively self-contained enclave of deprived and
possibly pathological individuals (cf. Moynihan, 1965;

Lewis, 1966). This poverty culture is seen as virtually autonomous, self-perpetuating, and self-defeating by contributing to the failure of the poor to live up to mainstream ideals (Leacock, 1971:12). Jones suggests that a similar view of the poor is found, although to a lesser extent, in approaches to poverty which emphasize the situational factors affecting the values and behavior of the poor (cf. Liebow, 1967; Hannerz, 1969). These studies do refer to the impact of urban and national institutions on the life of the poor, but as an afterthought or as static variables which can be mentioned and then ignored.

Traditional theories about collective behavior found in both the anthropological (e.g., Aberle, 1965; Wallace, 1956) and sociological (e.g., Gurr, 1970; Smelser, 1963) literature have also contributed to the general neglect of contextual factors. These early studies were largely social psychological approaches which focused on the individual and assumed that discontent and deprivation among a disorganized or aggrieved population provided the primary stimulus for the emergence of a social movement. Thus the central analytical features of movements were changes in the individual participant's values and attitudes and the resources and labor which participants could bring to the movement; the external environment of the movement was seen as unimportant and given a summary descriptive or historical treatment (McCarthy & Zald, 1977:1216-17). Gerlach and Hine's (1970:xiii) work and a number of recent case studies, however, cast doubt on the traditional assumption that a close link exists between discontent and the rise of a social movement. One result of this new data has been the development of the "resource mobilization" approach (e.g., Gamson, 1975; Tilly, 1975). This perspective focuses not on movement participants, but on both societal support and constraint on the activities of social movements (McCarthy & Zald, 1977:1213-14):

> It examines the variety of resources that must be mobilized, the linkages of social movements to other groups, the dependence of movements upon external support for success, and the tactics used by authorities to control or incorporate movements. . .[and] assumes that there is always enough discontent in any society to

138

supply the grass-roots support for a movement
if the movement is effectively organized and has
at its disposal the power and resources of some
established elite group.

These are the same issues raised by Gerlach and Hine's
(1973:184) model, particularly in their discussion of
the factors of organization and opposition. They
analyze cooperation and competition between movement
organizations for external resources, followers, and
public attention as an aspect of the organization, or
"extra-movement linkages," of a social movement. These
linkages are crucial for recruitment to many movements,
but more importantly constitute ways in which sympathetic nonparticipants can be contacted for financial
and other forms of aid. These ties link the movement
infrastructure to the overall structure of the established social system within which the movement exists,
and help participants deal with the system to their
own advantage (Gerlach & Hine, 1970:61-2). Their
model also places a great deal of emphasis on the opposition which a movement inevitably generates within
some segments of the larger society. The resource
mobilization literature has urged observers to take
into account the importance of costs (as well as rewards) in explaining individual and organizational
willingness to become involved in social movement
activity as well (McCarthy & Zald, 1977:1216). The
Gerlach-Hine model, however, assumes that risk and
opposition act not only as constraints on social
movement activity, but also have positive effects.
In particular they suggest that an optimum amount of
opposition (short of effective total social control
or annihilation of the movement) can always be turned
to the advantage of a movement by serving as a basis
for the commitment process and as a force against
which to unite its disparate segments.

A great deal of material has already been provided in
earlier chapters on the sources of support and opposition for the various Welfare Mothers Movement groups
in Minnesota. This information will be drawn together
in the first three sections of this chapter which focus on the public or formal groups that provided support or opposition to the AFDC League and MWRO and on
the tactics used by welfare officials and others to
control the movement. In addition, a pragmatic or covert way in which movement groups were linked to

external resources and groups will be described. The use of this "intermedial process" will be analyzed to determine the types of people involved, the situations in which such activities occurred and the reasons for its importance for movement groups.

Real and Imagined Opposition

Gerlach and Hine (1970:183-97) point out that social movements always consist of groups with different goals and tactics--each of which generates varying levels of opposition from different segments of the established order. They urge observers to be aware that opposition, as understood by a movement participant, is relative to his or her own personal position in the existing social structure and particular set of values. In other words, participants who face only censure or ostracism for their involvement may, from an outsider's point of view, seem to be facing less risk than a participant in another group who runs the risk of being the victim of police brutality or arrests. Yet from the perspective of those people whose reputations have been of deep concern all their lives and who are deeply committed to mainstream values, public ridicule may act as effectively to deter participation as the threat of an arrest. The dynamic that motivates movement growth, therefore, depends not only on the amount of "real" opposition or the type of risk, but also on participants' subjective perception of these costs. Movement groups also differ in the kind of real opposition they generate. As Gerlach and Hine (1973:185) point out, groups which seek only integration of oppressed minorities into the mainstream of American life may cause opposition but their goals demand no radical restructuring of our society, only social mobility for a heretofore excluded category of people. When claims by minorities are modified to include a call for the total elimination of poverty, however, this constitutes a far more revolutionary goal and such groups tend to experience heightened opposition from wider segments of the society.

The two major Welfare Mothers Movement groups in Minnesota were found to vary in the risk and opposition, real or imagined, they faced. There were several institutions and categories of people in the larger society which were generally perceived as

140

potential opponents who might work to defeat the
goals of a movement group at any particular point in
time. The AFDC League and MWRO chose different institutions from this set of opponents as the key target
for most of their political activities, however, not
only because of their own ideology, but also because
the differing political contexts facing the two groups
had a major impact on the availability of resources
for protest activities.

Opposing institutions and groups. Most of the welfare
mothers moved beyond focusing their anger at specific
individuals, such as social workers, after participating in a movement organization. It was acknowledged
that some workers might have personal motives for
"putting recipients down," but most were not seen as
enemies. Rather the women began to perceive the welfare institution itself as one of the key groups which
actually controlled the distribution of welfare and
other resources on the local and national levels. In
other words, the administrators and not the workers
were perceived as the real source of opposition to
the movement. Informants also stated that the legislative branch of the government was, if not hostile,
at least indifferent to the goals of movement groups.
Both the predominantly conservative Minnesota state
legislators and members of Congress were believed to
be far more concerned with the reactions of taxpayers
to a welfare issue than they were likely to be responsive to the desires of welfare mothers. AFDC League
members were especially likely to be aware of the
opposition welfare mothers could expect from legislators, having spent a great deal more time in lobbying
efforts than had MWRO or other movement groups in the
state. Finally, the general public was perceived by
many participants to be opposed to the poor in general
and the Welfare Mothers Movement in particular. Welfare mothers often identified categories of people
with whom they had daily contact, such as store own-
ers, landlords, and sometimes the "rich" or the
"middle class" as hostile to the movement.

In addition to these institutions, one organized group
of opponents called Wonderful Opportunities, Rewards
Keen (WORK) emerged in Minnesota. This group was
formed in reaction to what its members saw as the
general liberalizing trends in the giving of public
welfare during the 1960s, and the increased militancy

and visibility of movement groups such as MWRO. Thus
the major activity of WORK members involved appearing
at MWRO demonstrations and hearings to dispute their
demands for increased grant levels and for other reforms designed to lessen the indignity associated
with receiving welfare. WORK was part of a larger
"countermovement" (McCarthy & Zald, 1977:1218), which
included a local tax reform group--the T Party, a
divorce reform group, an antifluoridation group, and
anticommunist organizations. The divorce reform
group was the oldest and in fact had had contact with
the AFDC League several years before. The AFDC League
had invited a spokesman from the group to present
their views that men were discriminated against by the
divorce laws and by obligatory alimony payments and
the automatic granting of child custody to the mother
after divorce proceedings. Their position on this
issue stemmed from a general belief that many divorced
women were promiscuous, neglected their children,
did not work even if they were able, and so were not
deserving of support. The members of the divorce reform group never made any attempt to harass or oppose
the legislative activities of the AFDC League, however, as the later WORK group did vis-a-vis MWRO.

Despite their frequent experience with desertion or
divorce, the welfare mothers participating in movement
groups did not specify males as a general category
which could be expected to oppose the Welfare Mothers
Movement; nor were men barred from joining movement
organizations (particularly after membership in MWRO
was expanded to include the working poor). The mothers
focus on class as opposed to gender conflict was in
line with the ideology of movement groups and the
women's commitment to traditional sex roles as described in Chapter Five.

The AFDC League. From an objective point of view,
AFDC League members faced less real opposition than
did MWRO. This was due in part to their goals such
as self-help, which did not challenge mainstream cultural beliefs in the ability of Americans to pull
themselves up by their bootstraps and which were not
a threat to the existing economic or political power
structure. For example, the group's legislative
goals were modest in scope, not designed to be financially burdensome, and were to be achieved through
conventional political activities. AFDC League

142

participants often feared reprisals from individual social workers for their participation in the group, but only the more sophisticated leaders saw the welfare department as a major opposition group. They did so because they believed the support given the AFDC League by welfare officials and their early help in formulating the group's legislative reforms were cynical attempts to coopt the movement or to allow welfare mothers to let off steam without having to bear the brunt of the women's protest themselves.

AFDC League members were unanimous, however, in emphasizing the risk they believed was involved in their participation in the group. They were afraid of the reactions of their social workers or of potential backlash from the public in the form of harassment by strangers who would call a welfare mother whose name had been in the paper and subject her to verbal abuse. For these women, who were trying to better their lives and become upwardly mobile, this kind of attack was especially painful. They feared the reaction of state legislators, who might see their participation in the political process as illegitimate, for although there is no legal basis for it, many Americans unconsciously believe that individuals who do not conform to mainstream American values or who accept public welfare aid forfeit many of their rights as citizens.[1] By lobbying and playing the rules of the game, however, the women hoped to establish that they were different from other recipients and not only capable, but worthy, of political participation. In other words, many welfare mothers were not aware of the generally supportive climate of opinion which had emerged in the mid-1960s among government officials, elites and other significant segments of the larger society (cf. Piven & Cloward, 1971). Only the more active leaders and staff members of movement groups were truly aware of the potential for support--that many groups were "trying to change their image, to become meaningful to the whole community and not just the middle class," as June Waldheim put it.

MWRO. The appearance of MWRO marked a dramatic change in the relationship between organized welfare recipients and the welfare system. This new focus on the welfare department as the target institution stemmed from the assumption of NWRO strategists, such as Piven and Cloward, that the welfare system was particularly vulnerable to protest at this point in time. They believed that the Civil Rights Movement and riots in major Northern cities had created a climate in which the federal government might be willing to make concessions to the poor. The tactics chosen to fight a bureaucratic organization such as the welfare department were disruptive mass actions, sit-ins and demonstrations by large numbers of welfare mothers, which would shut down the operation of the department and force welfare officials to grant their demands for increased benefits to those already on welfare and for reform of the entire welfare system. These goals and tactics inevitably led to dramatic public conflict and direct confrontation with welfare administrators. The need not only to create conflict, but to exacerbate it, can be seen in the statement of an NWRO organizer who counseled MWRO members to remember:

> You're demonstrating to build an organization and power--so no one is "nice" on the outside except when you're finally at home. Organizationally, they must always be wrong.

NWRO's alternate (although less publicized) tactic involved using the courts to establish the illegality of some of the worst administrative practices and to force conformance with existing welfare statutes. WRO leaders and staff on both the national and local levels worked closely with lawyers in developing the issues and cases which were to be taken to court, and many of their most notable successes were achieved through litigation. The threat of possible legal action was also considered if protest tactics failed, as when MWRO demonstrated against the flat grant system while at the same time warning they could legally delay implementation of the new plan on the grounds of a legal technicality. These legal challenges were not used to generate publicity for movement goals or to inform the public of the larger political issues surrounding the case, but were designed in a straightforward manner to effect a change in the laws. Thus, the courts were not perceived as a major target institution by the welfare mothers (although they were used in this way by the antiwar and antinuclear movements described by Barkan, 1979:30-3). The failure to use the legal system in this way was due in large part to movement ideology, as Sam Putnam pointed out:

I have the power to make some very basic changes
in the welfare system through the Legal Aid
Society in Minnesota. In November of 1969, one
of our lawsuits wiped out the three months
waiting period to establish eligibility for
AFDC. Okay, it makes a great difference; it
cost the state a lot of money. The problem is
that it is very elitest--a bunch of lawyers
were here and poor people were sure lucky. A
lot of welfare mothers' lives were changed by
our lawsuit but they didn't know how it happened.
The system never changed as far as they were
concerned.

MWRO's militancy also provoked strong reactions from
some segments of the general public which already
opposed the public welfare system and affected the
kind of press coverage given the movement. MWRO leaders were by no means oblivious to the value of good
publicity as a means of generating public support for
their demands. Yet in spite of the group's efforts
to prepare press releases stressing MWRO's goals, news
coverage tended to focus on the drama of disruption
rather than on the issue at hand.

During MWRO's second year in Minnesota, however, the
focus and tactics of the organization changed a great
deal. In response to initiatives coming from national
strategists, MWRO moved from a single to a multi-issue
organization using a wider variety of tactics. The
new focus had three related thrusts: (1) the extension of WRO membership eligibility and the development
of issues of interest to the working poor; (2) the
building of alliances with other groups and human
rights movements; and (3) an interest in electoral
politics within the Democratic Party and a willingness
to use conventional lobbying to help defeat FAP in
the Congress. Although the faction within NWRO led
by Piven and Cloward objected to this change in tactics on the grounds that welfare mothers had no means
of exerting conventional political influence, a majority of NWRO leaders welcomed the chance to move from
the initial phase of "people power" into a period of
"people politics."

Following NWRO's lead, MWRO turned its attention to
new target institutions and to nonwelfare issues, such
as the Title I campaign to use federal school funds

to buy winter clothing for poor children. Aware of
the increasingly antiwelfare mood of the state and
the nation, MWRO leaders planned large demonstrations
to initiate a campaign, but the intransigence was
gone. Whereas before any attempts by officials to
negotiate had been vehemently opposed, they were now
welcomed once the initial confrontation had brought
the issue to public attention. The Minnesota State
Legislature became a major source of opposition for
MWRO at this time as well. MWRO responded to the
threat of welfare reductions by developing "middle-
class" tactics such as lobbying in order to avoid
antagonizing legislators and, for the first time,
agreed to become part of a broad coalition of establishment and social movement groups which could bring
additional pressure to bear on the legislature in
order to defeat the proposal.

As McCarthy and Zald (1977:1222) point out, authorities or opponents of movement groups do not always
act in concert. Thus as the focus of opposition for
MWRO shifted from the welfare system to other institutions, regular meetings between MWRO leaders and the
new director of the Hennepin County Welfare Department
were instituted. More importantly, MWRO and the county
welfare department were both opposed to the proposed
welfare reductions and actually began to plan a coordinated campaign against the state welfare system and
legislature. Thus former opponents had become allies
due to the financial crises of the 1970s.

Given the obvious impact which the authorities and
other opposing institutions had on the activities and
goals of movement organizations, it is important to
take a closer look at the various tactics they used
to control or oppose the movement.

Responses of the Authorities and Opposition Groups

The welfare system on both the county and state levels perceived and responded to the AFDC League and
MWRO in quite different ways. This difference was
due in large part to the goals and tactics of the
two groups and in part to changes within the welfare
department itself. For example, Eugene Heber, the
director of the Hennepin County Welfare Department
through 1970, was trained in social work and had been

with the public welfare system since its beginning
in the Great Depression. Heber had very positive
feelings about the earlier AFDC League and characterized that organization in this way during an interview:

> The AFDC Mothers League (sic) was a more local-
> ized, spontaneous, amateurish effort on the
> part of AFDC recipients. . . to develop a vehi-
> cle for communicating with the county welfare
> department and the state DPW as a group of
> people with common concerns and interests. Our
> relationship was a very amicable, cooperative,
> relaxed one in which we cooperated with them
> by providing technical speakers to their meet-
> ings, etc.

Statements by several officials suggest that they were
aware of the ultimate consequence (whether originally
intended or not) of their cooperation with the AFDC
League. One welfare administrator, for example,
pointed out that the department's support of the AFDC
League enhanced the department's public image as a
responsive government agency and, by referring to the
democratic ideal of "citizen participation," served
to legitimize the department's own program for legislative change. At the same time, from an observer's
point of view, an additional benefit of encouraging
the AFDC League's legislative activities was that this
focus kept the pressure on elected officials rather
than on the welfare system.

In contrast, Heber perceived MWRO's later actions as
"manufactured, fictitious issues in many instances"
which were fomented in Minnesota by "skillful, trained,
professional outside agitators." One of the department's younger administrators pointed out that Heber's
background had predisposed him toward taking a strong
stand against MWRO because he was basically "status
quo, conservative, 'protect the integrity of the dol-
lar' [and motivated by a] 'look at the fine service
we are providing these poor people'" attitude. Thus
Heber over-reacted to MWRO's militancy, formulated a
new county policy which made it explicitly illegal to
remain in the department after closing time and then
called in the police to arrest demonstrators after two
days of sit-ins during the 1969 clothing campaign. Thus
the pattern of interaction between MWRO and local welfare officials was one of confrontation and escalation.

John Frederick was hired as the new director for the
Hennepin County Welfare Department in 1971. He made
an effort to familiarize himself with NWRO literature
before taking his new job and attended a meeting of
the Minnesota Friends of Welfare Rights soon after
moving to the state. His hiring coincided with
MWRO's orientation toward nonwelfare issues and lobbying tactics and he was, therefore, never confronted
with any militant demonstrations at the welfare department. Yet, in spite of his own opposition to the
proposed welfare cutbacks, he too was angry at the
"aggressive" way in which MWRO speakers acted at public hearings and stated that he had sympathized with
state welfare officials over the "indignities" they
had suffered at the hands of MWRO members. (From the
perspective of the militant demonstrations of a year
before, of course, their behavior had been quite re-
strained.) Frederick was also quick to take offense
at any hint of militancy from MWRO leaders, often misread their jocular bantering as veiled threats, and
responded with threats of his own.

The statements of the welfare officials whom I interviewed and who spoke at MWRO demonstrations suggest
that they reacted negatively to MWRO because the group
used new, unpredictable, and from their point of view,
improper tactics. The illegitimacy of the welfare
mothers' actions sprang from: (1) their creation of
a public conflict focused on the welfare department
itself--an institution dedicated to confidentiality
and service to its clients, and (2) their use of
resources from outside the local political arena, such
as community organizers, militant churchmen, and poverty lawyers to influence the decisions of the welfare
bureaucracy which before had only been subject to
internal review and appeal. The dilemma which faced
the officials of a public agency as a result of the
tactics and negative publicity generated by MWRO was
quite evident in the statement of this welfare official:

> I think that probably the image of the AFDC
> League was more positive among the staff than
> that of WRO primarily because of their own pub-
> lic relations attitudes. How they operated had
> some bearing on it. The AFDC League took a fair-
> ly aggressive but good PR attitude towards work-
> ing with the community, with the welfare depart-
> ment, or with the legislature--trying to promote

good relationships through the system, so to speak, so they could accomplish their objectives. . . . But on the other hand, the WRO took a very aggressive, very militant stand with the welfare department as an organization. The Welfare Rights group had a real session here a year and a half ago on a drive for greater clothing allowances, and some of the leadership were pretty aggressive gals, almost physical in the way they proceeded. We had some sit-ins in the welfare department. We had police complaints, people being charged with criminal activities, that sort of thing. So I think that although there was a lot of sympathy toward their objectives among the staff, there was real distress with the methods used. I think this was probably the most common feeling, almost an antagonism toward those methods. We knew that maybe our clothing allowances should be better --they were awfully hard to live on. But is this the way to get better clothing allowances? . . . We've got to get the community to support us and you don't get community support by having sit-ins and that sort of thing.

As a result of their opposition to MWRO, groups such as the welfare department developed a set of justifications for their actions. The use of these statements were aimed as much at the public in an attempt to undermine support for movement goals, as they were at movement participants. The following three themes were most often used to defend the welfare officials' opposition to MWRO's demands: (1) we are objective, rational, and acting in the best interests of welfare mothers and the public as a whole; (2) "I had a tough row to hoe, too" (i.e., others have seen hard times, such as the Depression, and made it through, so why should welfare mothers be making demands for better grant levels); and (3) we are interested in establishing a dialogue, whereas MWRO deliberately tries to obscure and polarize issues on which we actually have a lot in common.

In addition to these normative justifications of their denial of movement demands, the welfare officials also frequently used a variety of pragmatic tactics to frustrate MWRO in particular: (1) by passing the buck (within or between levels of government) or claiming

lack of authority to deal with an issue; (2) by refusing to deal with MWRO (a) because it was not "representative" of all welfare mothers in the city or
state, or (b) because of the confidentiality of client
records (which Silberman, 1964, suggests can be used
as a "conspiracy of silence" designed to block inves-
tigation of client/worker relations in some cases);
(3) by co-opting leaders through appointment to an
advisory board or through the offer of a job or job
training; (4) by gathering information about the intended actions of a welfare group in order to plan
their own response or undercut the group's demands;
and (5) through the use of negative sanctions such
as arrest or the threat of termination of benefits.

MWRO's use of confrontation and demonstrations was
less effective against the county school board and
the private building contractor selected as the target of their housing campaign in 1971 than it had
been against the welfare department. Both these
groups were sensitive to the effects of bad publicity
and potentially vulnerable to the exposure of ques-
tionable practices, such as the misuse of federal
Title I funds (see chap. 3, note 1) or the building
of middle-income housing in areas already experiencing a low-income housing crisis. MWRO was not able
to generate any public or working-class support for
their demands, however, and did not have the resources
which were needed to prove either of the groups had
acted illegally or unethically. School board members
could easily reject MWRO's proposed use of Title I
money for school clothing on the grounds that such a
use would violate federal rules (although the rules
were actually ambiguous in this regard) and because
they had to consider the needs of all their constituents, not just the poor. The building contractor
successfully opposed MWRO's demands that some of his
units be rented at reduced rates to the poor on the
grounds that our American system of private enterprise guaranteed him the right to conduct his business
as he wished. Since welfare recipients had no special
relationship with these groups and since they were not
physically able to disrupt the functioning of the
school system or the firm's construction sites, both
of these campaigns were easily contained by the target institution. The limited success which resulted
from the Title I campaign was not directly the result
of MWRO's actions, but due to the concessions of what

150

McCarthy and Zald (1977:1223) call the "conscience elite." Convinced of the validity of MWRO's claim that poor children could not properly clothe themselves for school, a school board member who also belonged to the Urban Coalition pressured that group into allotting $10,000 to school social workers to be distributed to needy children in the county, thereby indirectly accomplishing MWRO's goal.

Support and Alliances

As the above example shows, the support of elite groups which could channel financial and other resources to movement organizations was crucial to the success or failure of specific activities in many instances. Relations between Welfare Mothers Movement groups and outside organizations were, therefore, not solely antagonistic, despite the opposition the welfare mothers perceived from many segments of the larger society and the intransigent statements of the more militant groups such as MWRO.

The AFDC League's goals of changing the public image of the welfare mother and influencing welfare legislation required that the relatively powerless and stigmatized welfare mothers actively seek the support of a wide variety of organizations. Most of these were traditional establishment women's organizations, social work groups, and parapolitical community organizations such as the Urban Coalition. These external groups controlled resources which they could make available to the AFDC League--particularly funding, labor, political influence, and legitimacy.

In addition to the help of the county welfare departments described earlier, informants suggested that two organizations had played particularly important roles in the AFDC League's history. The YWCA gave the fledgling group permission to use its facilities for meetings, the printing of fliers, etc. June Waldheim believed that such support from an established and respected organization had demonstrated that the AFDC League was not just a "bunch of kooks" and had also enabled her to work with the organization as an unpaid staff person because of her job as Adult Activities Coordinator with the YWCA. The National Association of Social Workers (NASW) had been instrumental in helping the AFDC League to expand as well by providing financial support for welfare mothers to travel to other counties around the state in order to speak about the group's goals and organize new chapters. In addition, the NASW loaned the services of its professional lobbyist to the AFDC League for the 1966-67 legislative session--the only year in which part of the group's legislative reform package was enacted into law.

Favorable publicity was also considered vital to the achievement of the AFDC League's goals and one of the major ways of informing isolated welfare mothers about the existence of the organization. Publicity and opportunities to speak at the meetings of other community organizations were major avenues for reaching the public with the AFDC League's message that many welfare mothers were committed to mainstream values, for forming contacts with influential people, and occasionally for developing direct support for the AFDC League's legislative program as well.

While the leaders of the AFDC League actively sought the support of a wide variety of groups, they were also wary that an outside organization might attempt to dominate the welfare mothers. As a result, only one official support group was established by the AFDC League in 1968. This was a short-lived advisory board whose members were drawn from a number of local community organizations in Minneapolis. The group was to serve as "allies, not leaders" and were to react to the AFDC League's ideas for new legislation. The only time this advisory board was used, however, was when its members helped the AFDC League draw up bylaws in accordance with correct parliamentary procedure.

The AFDC League also did not form any alliances with other social movements of the decade. Nor did the leaders, members, or staff of the AFDC League have many personal contacts with participants in other movements. In interviews, most AFDC League members showed only minimal interest in the actions of Civil Rights, Antiwar, or Women's Liberation Movement groups. The one exception to this generalization was their backing of the equal pay and liberalized abortion programs advocated by Women's Liberation groups. Even here, however, the women tempered their support for this latter change by pointing out they feared such a law might

lead to increased sexual promiscuity. Informants
attributed this lack of interest in alliances with
other movements to the kind of women who joined the
AFDC League and to the organization's goals. The
group was well over half white, and those black women
who joined were interested in welfare, not racial
problems. In addition, the women were committed to
mainstream values and conventional behavior, yet were
most likely to be aware of the radical goals and actions of other social movements which attracted the
attention of the press. Thus a group which strove to
change the negative public image of the welfare mother
was unlikely to ally itself with, for example, Women's
Liberation groups which appeared not only to support
equal pay for women, but also to engage in bra-burning
or espouse lesbianism and other radical goals.

In general, then, the AFDC League was fairly successful in securing verbal public support and approval,
but less able to develop real support for legislative
reform from outside the social work community. As
June Waldheim put it:

> I think the funniest part about the AFDC League
> is that it had the greatest prestige outside of
> itself. I mean government people, OEO, social
> workers--all looked to the AFDC League as a real
> gung ho thing. The women in the AFDC League
> often. . . didn't think the organization was
> accomplishing anything, but they did have a
> great deal of prestige in the community.

The experience of Welfare Rights Organizations were
different, however. Piven and Cloward (1977:320-22)
have suggested that initially both white and black
leaders were ambivalent about supporting a welfare
organization because they were fighting to get
jobs for poor blacks, not get them on welfare. After
these early misgivings, however, three kinds of resources became available to NWRO. First, Civil Rights
groups, the leaders of several national religious de-
nominations, and some segments of the social welfare
profession began to accept the idea that people had a
"right" to welfare. This ideological support conferred
a certain amount of legitimacy on the organization.
Second, external groups provided NWRO with the appearance (it not always the reality) of possessing conventional political influence. Thus NWRO leaders and

staff were invited to attend conferences, speak before establishment organizations, and provide input on welfare policy issues within the federal government. Third, NWRO began to receive financial support from foundations, other movement organizations, and even the federal government (when the Department of Labor contracted with NWRO to monitor the implementation of local employment and training programs being offered to welfare mothers). This type of contribution made frequent regional and national meetings of recipients and organizers possible and enabled NWRO to hire a large national staff. The private institution which clearly provided the most assistance to NWRO was the church, however. Churchmen and religious groups which had been affected by the Civil Rights Movement became strong supporters of WRO groups; local churches provided money, office space, telephones, and other kinds of equipment for producing WRO literature.

In Minnesota, similar local-level resources were made available to MWRO. The major differences between MWRO and the earlier AFDC League, then, were: (1) the amount of financial support which MWRO was able to gather, and (2) the more radical segments of the community which offered their time and money to a militant Welfare Mothers Movement group. These differences enabled MWRO to hire a full-time staff and to broaden their demands for change with less concern for their public image or the responses of conventional establishment groups. Radical students volunteered to help organize MWRO locals and antiwar, feminist and socialist literature competed for space with NWRO fliers in the organization's office. A church on the Southside of Minneapolis, a local church federation, and the Urban Coalition provided the financial resources. Direct grants of several thousands of dollars were given to pay an organizer's salary and buy office materials, and VISTA volunteers allotted to these groups were turned over to MWRO for their use.

Just as important as this logistic support was the legitimacy the clergy in the state provided. This support helped convince not only the welfare mothers but also some outsiders that what MWRO was demanding had some justification in our moral and religious principles. The following excerpt from Carl Jones' statement at a public hearing illustrates this kind of support:

In a time when we are visited by a guest that is not altogether welcome--inflation--those of us in society who have jobs and are employed usually have some kind of compensation for this guest in our lives. Welfare recipients do not have that kind of compensation and now you are considering taking away even part of that which they do have. I think the situation is parallel to one of our stories from the Judaeo-Christian tradition. It is the story of David and Bathsheba, where David sent Uriah, Bathsheba's husband, out into the front of battle so that he might have Bathsheba. The prophet of the land, a man by the name of Nathan, came to David, telling him this story: "There were two men who lived in a city; one was rich and the other was poor. The rich man had many flocks. The poor man had only his small family and one ewe lamb that he bought and raised in his home like it was a part of his family. A guest came to visit the rich man and he was ' loathe to take a lamb from his own flock and so he took the small ewe lamb from the poor man, slew it, prepared it, and fed the guest." David was in anger and said, "The man who has done this shall die and he shall pay for it fourfold." Nathan said to David, "You are the man." The Friends of Welfare Rights declare today that the poor must not be made to offer up their small portion in order to meet the financial crises of the 1970s.

Although they accepted the support of activist groups, MWRO staff members did not seek the help of small community groups and women's organizations which the AFDC League had cultivated. In fact, on the few occasions when overtures from establishment groups such as the NAACP were made, their offers of support were ignored. Certainly no help was given MWRO by the county welfare departments and the only reaction by social work organizations in the state was to invite MWRO speakers to give workshops at their conventions.

The Friends of Welfare Rights. Soon after MWRO was formed, Carl Jones and several social work professionals from the area began building a formal auxiliary organization for nonrecipients wishing to support MWRO. The Friends group, as it was called, managed to attract a great deal of early publicity for MWRO through their initial "Live on a Welfare Budget" campaign. Members of the Friends, as well as a number of local influentials such as then Senator Walter Mondale participated in this campaign (although he did not join the Friends of Welfare Rights). At the end of a week of existing solely on a welfare budget, sympathetic stories telling of the difficulties and privations the families had experienced were reported in the local press. Senator Mondale (personal communication, March, 1970) later pointed out, however, that his participation in this media event had led to a number of irate phone calls to his home in Minneapolis in which he had been berated for his involvement in the campaign and which complained about welfare in general.

In accordance with NWRO policy, the Friends of Welfare Rights in Minnesota consisted of a set of officers and a large body of members who were to help support the actions of MWRO. Members were primarily liberal social workers, clergymen, and students (from the School of Social Work at the nearby university). The function of the group was to contribute financially to MWRO's operation through the $10-15 yearly dues, and to "speak to their own kind" (i.e., to friends, co-workers, and laymen from the middle class), explaining MWRO's position on issues such as Nixon's Family Assistance Plan. In addition, the Friends group was to provide support for MWRO activities by demonstrating along with the welfare mothers, writing letters and telephoning influential acquaintances in the state, and serving as baby-sitters or drivers for the welfare mothers during demonstrations. Although members of the Friends group described the interpretive, proselytizing activity as their primary concern, the welfare mothers consistently emphasized their use for more immediate services, such as baby-sitting. These activities were not very personally rewarding for most Friends, however, and resulted in a great deal of disaffection within the group.

This loose structure and the lack of a clear set of ongoing tasks for the Friends was well-suited to the erratic nature of MWRO's campaigns. Such an informal organization was also deliberately designed, however, to ensure that the Friends could not develop into an independent group which might attempt to exert influence on the recipient leaders of MWRO. While this

structure may have solved the general problem of conflicts between elite supporters and indigeneous leaders over the control of movement organizations
which has been reported elsewhere in the literature
(McCarthy & Zald, 1977:1231), it created a further
dilemma for MWRO. Many of the early (and most enthusiastic) members of the Friends complained that the
MWRO leaders and staff never gave them any direction
or specific action on which they could work in between campaigns. Thus most of the members soon
dropped out of the group, leaving the chairperson as
the only visible representative of the Friends at
MWRO actions. The dilemma of creating a formal
group of supporters but then denying then any authority to set their own goals was clearly evident at a
meeting in 1970. Leslie Bernstein, MWRO's organizer,
had asked Carl Jones to set up a meeting with one of
the social work professors at the university in order
to develop plans to get the Friends group going
again. Carl, Leslie, and a number of MWRO leaders
attended the meeting. Carl described what happened:

> I made some statements there about doing this
> or that--mounting a membership/fund-raising
> drive and enlarging the group by extending mem-
> bership eligibility to include organizations
> as well as individuals. But when we got out,
> Rita Jarvis said, "What do you mean, we'll do
> this or that? The mothers haven't decided
> this." She really put me down because I had
> made some assumptions and in a sense violated
> the mothers' freedom to make decisions. I felt
> a little bit put out by her being angry though
> because the assumptions I had made were about
> the Friends, and not the mothers. I thought
> since I was chairman of the Friends that I had
> some authority to make some of these decisions.

MWRO alliances. Despite the fact that many of MWRO's
volunteer staff members in 1969 (such as students and
VISTAs) were personally involved in a number of other
social movement groups, MWRO as an organization and
MWRO members themselves did not participate in or
establish alliances with those movements. The reasons given for this by MWRO members were very similar
to those of the AFDC League participants; they verbally supported the moderate goals of other human
rights movements, but were a little put off by some

157

of their more radical actions and felt they had little to gain personally from such groups. Their immediate concerns were welfare problems, not sex
roles or racism. NWRO was not anxious to form alliances with other groups at this time, in order to
establish itself as an independent organization with
distinct goals; nor were leaders in the antiwar,
feminist, and civil rights movements initially interested in allying themselves with a welfare mothers
organization (Piven & Cloward, 1977:320).

As NWRO's legitimacy grew, however, and as the organization began to focus increasingly on lobbying
against FAP, it began to actively recruit links with
"sister organizations." These were social movements
representing a broad spectrum of disadvantaged minorities, which were actively engaged in "getting
people their rights." Some of the more prominent
organizations which became linked with NWRO causes
and which sent representatives to NWRO conventions
were the National Tenants Union, the National Organization for Women, the Southern Christian Leadership
Conference, and ethnic movements such as La Raza
and the American Indian Movement. The existence of
such alliances on the national level were not binding
on WRO affiliates, although they were encouraged to
establish local ties with groups from these various
movements if they could be of potential use to the
welfare rights struggle in their own community.

In Minnesota, the need for broad support from a variety of groups arose in the spring of 1971 when the
state legislature attempted to cut the welfare budget
by 10%. The initial stimulus for this coalition,
however, actually came from an activist social workers' association formed that year, called the Minnesota 87 (for the number of counties in the state).
This new group approached MWRO representatives and
the few remaining active members of the AFDC League
who were attending the 1971 Minnesota Welfare Association conference. The Minnesota 87 leaders urged
MWRO and the AFDC League to join together to defeat
the proposed cut, offered their support, and began
contacting other groups which might wish to participate in the coalition. The number of organizations
involved in the coalition grew rapidly to include
not only the two Welfare Mothers Movement groups and
the Minnesota 87, but also religious and ecumenical

groups, the National Association of Social Workers, the Legal Aid Society, the Urban League, groups of senior citizens, the American Indian Movement, OEO-affiliated organizations such as Model Cities and Pilot Cities, the Minneapolis Tenants Union, the League of Women Voters, the AFL-CIO, and the Urban Coalition. Each of these organizations as well as several county welfare departments sent representatives to protest the proposed reduction in the welfare budget at public hearings in the state capital.

Given the broad range of groups which were asked or chose to join the coalition, groups from the Women's Liberation Movement were conspicuous by their absence. Those women's organizations, such as the League of Women Voters, which did participate in the public hearing were the same groups which had supported the earlier lobbying efforts of the AFDC League and were involved in conventional political, rather than feminist, issues. In other words, welfare was not at that time perceived as a woman's issue either by welfare mothers or by women from other social classes. The potential for solidarity on the basis of sex was ignored in favor of solidarity among low-status groups which could be expected to have dealings with the welfare system, such as the aged, blacks, and American Indians. These movement organizations were perceived as helpful but not particularly influential by local welfare mothers; traditional or establishment groups and speakers from the social work community were the most effective kind of supporter. The staff, on the other hand, tended to rely most heavily on more militant social action groups, such as the Tenants Union, and religious organizations.

All groups in the coalition were watched, however, to ensure that the welfare mothers remained in control at the hearings and that the tactics, demands, or suggestions made had received MWRO's prior approval. The staff in particular warned MWRO's leaders that even the most well-meaning supporter might "sell MWRO down the river" in negotiations by reaching an agreement, binding on all parties, which was not in MWRO's or the welfare mothers' best interests. There was also concern that other social movement organizations might attempt to "rip MWRO off" by advancing their own cause without a return commitment to MWRO's goals. In the end, MWRO leaders hoped that by maintaining a high profile at the hearings, whatever political credit might accrue from a successful stand against the proposed cutback would flow to MWRO rather than another organization.

Intermediaries[2]

The visible activities which have so far been the focus of attention in this chapter--the formal alliances, public support given Welfare Mothers Movement groups, and the dramatic opposition of WORK, the legislators, or welfare department were by no means the only way in which movement groups were linked with supporters and opponents. A limited number of nonrecipients (June Waldheim with the AFDC League, and from MWRO Tina Czernek, Leslie Bernstein, Carl Jones, and Sam Putnam) were also involved in less obvious ways in gathering support or dealing with opposition groups. These individuals all had publicly acknowledged tasks linking their organizations with particular resources or target populations but, in addition, used their positions to engage to varying degrees in what will here be called the intermedial process. Their actions often were a source of conflict within their movement group and were contrary to the normative rule that welfare mothers were to control all aspects of the internal and external political processes of their groups. An examination of the situations in which intermediation most frequently occurred will provide some explanation for the emergence and persistence of this largely covert political process within the movement.

Following Friedrich (1968:199-204) and Bailey (1969: 167-76), an intermediary may be described as a political specialist who interrelates the needs, aspirations, and/or traditions of a local-level group to the corresponding demands, resources or political-legal order of a larger encapsulating unit, such as a bureaucracy, city or state. The intermediary serves to link two or more groups with seemingly irreconcilable differences in resources, power, organization or culture. Not all roles found at the point of contact between such units are to be considered intermediaries, however. As Bailey (1969:167) states:

The local leader who fights resolutely and

single-mindedly for local autonomy is not a middleman nor is the bureaucrat who intends and who is able to wipe out the local structure. The essence of the role is to keep a foot in both camps.

In the abstract, intermedial activities are neutral processes; they are links which can be used openly or covertly either to bridge the gap between the smaller and larger structure or to politicize and widen the gap, thereby escalating intergroup conflict. As with all dynamic political processes, feedback occurs between changes in the political arena and the actions of the intermediary. Thus the role of an intermediary is not static, but flexible, ambiguous, and difficult to maintain over a long period of time. It may, in fact, disappear altogether if the monopoly of communication usually enjoyed by an intermediary breaks down through the establishment of more direct links between the smaller unit and the dominant political system (Bailey, 1969:175-6).

As was pointed out, the individuals who were to some degree involved in the intermedial process within the Welfare Mothers Movement in Minnesota held formal positions with their groups. June Waldheim was on the staff of the YWCA and assigned to work with the AFDC League; Tina, Leslie, Carl Jones and Sam Putnam held positions described in NWRO fliers respectively as "staff/community organizer," "Friend of WRO," and "lawyer." Ideally they were to contribute their technical skills to their organization, but in actuality, all had some influence on the political decisions made by their group as well. They were not influential people in their own right (i.e., "authorities"), but had access (or knew how to get access) to influentials and the external organizational, moral, or legal resources which their group required. Taken at face value, their tasks were simply those of external supporters of a group of relatively powerless and politically inexperienced welfare mothers. In addition to their activities within the group, however, each of these individuals was engaged behind the scenes in either bridging the gap between movement organizations and opponents or supporters, or further isolating them in an attempt to maintain pragmatic control of the group. The major factors affecting variation in intermedial activities were (1) the degree of segmentation and decentralization of each movement organization; (2) the preferences of the welfare mothers; (3) the actions of outsiders; and (4) the level of conflict within the political arena.

The segmentation of movement groups affected the intermedial process. As the Gerlach-Hine model suggests, such an organizational form has many advantages, but it also requires that a great deal of energy be expended in linking the local units together and to the larger society. The more decentralized and segmented the group, the more dependent it is upon individuals who are willing to link it to outside resources, and the more vulnerable it is to those who wish to control the flow of resources and block communication.

For example, June Waldheim pointed out that in the early years of AFDC League activity, the welfare mothers themselves had been very active in seeking the support of individuals and groups, particularly during legislative years. In between legislative sessions and after the AFDC League organization began to disintegrate into separate satellite groups, June took on more of these linking activities, however, due in part to her wide range of contacts through the YWCA. In addition, since there was no longer a well publicized set of officers, outsiders who wished to contact the AFDC League were forced to call June, in spite of the fact that all such contacts were supposed to be made directly to recipient leaders. June consistently tried to bridge the gap between the AFDC League and potential supporters or influential people in the city, however, and never used her position to block information or manipulate the decisions made by the welfare mothers.

The intermedial process may not have been well developed in the AFDC League, but it played an important part in MWRO. For example, Sam Putnam provided MWRO with the legal knowledge it needed to fight the welfare system, but he also acted informally as a link between MWRO and both supporters and opponents. During an interview, Putnam pointed out that his own "middle-class notion of a lawyer's duty" to be objective in informing his clients (the welfare mothers) about possible legal repercussions had brought him into conflict with MWRO's first organizer, Tina. She

162

had wanted him to minimize the danger involved in militant confrontations and thus act as an advocate for this kind of tactic. Putnam did act as an advocate in the courtroom when defending MWRO members against legal charges, but in all other contexts he chose to assume a neutral stance. He was thus free to state his support for MWRO's goals, yet also express understanding of the welfare officials' situation. Putnam had, in fact, begun to develop personal contacts with local welfare officials soon after he became involved with MWRO and described his relationship with them in this way:

> I carry on contacts with the Hennepin County Welfare Department and I do not always play a straight "WRO-is-always-right-and-you-are-always -wrong" role, which I suppose is the strongest advocate role. This is because I know some people high up in the administration of the welfare department. It is my political judgment that I should maintain those relationships.

As a result of these contacts, Putnam was privy to crucial information about events within the welfare department which were relevant to MWRO's campaigns. He was able to channel early warning of impending department rulings and develop support for MWRO within the welfare department as a result of his intermedial activities. The welfare mothers were not even aware of many of the contacts with welfare administrators which he used for the ultimate benefit of MWRO.

Carl Jones' activities as an intermediary resulted largely from his status as a minister. The anthropological literature is full of examples which show the close relationship between religion and political disputes in many societies (cf. Swartz, Turner, & Tuden, 1966:187-246). Specialized ritual offices have often been used to restrain conflict and to make peace both within and between groups. Jones' religious role undoubtedly played a part in enabling him to act as an effective intermediary bridging the gap between MWRO and opponents, particularly during periods of heightened conflict with the welfare system.

Tina Czernek, on the other hand, was structurally in a position to link MWRO with outside groups or supporters, but she did not do so consistently. Despite

the fact that the ideology of MWRO required that she
simply funnel information and offers of support to
recipient leaders, more often she blocked this kind
of information if she felt it came from an inappro-
priate source (e.g., an establishment as opposed to
radical organization) or if such contact would take
the time and energy of active leaders without giving
much to MWRO in return. Tina's personal characteristics (she had been on welfare, a member of a WRO
group in another city, and completely identified
with the WRO cause) and the intense conflict she was
instrumental in creating usually barred her from
acting as an intermediary who could link MWRO to
opposition groups, as Carl and Sam had. Rather
Tina acted in confrontations as a leader--giving
opinions, making ad hoc decisions, refusing to negotiate, and often voicing more militant demands than
the welfare mothers.

In contrast to Tina, Leslie did not openly engage
in leadership activities within MWRO, but she actually was more involved in the intermedial process.
This increased opportunity to act as an intermediary
arose in part because MWRO was in a state of flux
during the time Leslie was the group's organizer.
Officers changed several times, the group was no
longer able to pay for a central office, and for
long periods of time Leslie was the only visible
link between MWRO locals and between MWRO and outside groups. In addition, Leslie urged Carl Jones
to become less involved in MWRO and to stop attending
meetings on the grounds that (albeit unintentionally)
he had assumed too prominent a leadership role.
The pragmatic consequence of her suggestion, of
course, was to remove an alternate link between MWRO
and groups of opponents and supporters in the larger
society. Finally, during this year MWRO planned
several campaigns against groups other than the welfare department. Leslie's hand was strengthened by
this change in strategy because the welfare mothers,
while familiar with the welfare system by this time,
knew little about the legislature and other groups.

Both Tina and Leslie were supposed to link local welfare recipients to other organizations and to provide a free flow of information on which recipient
leaders could make informed decisions. In actuality,
however, most of their intermedial activities were

devoted to covertly blocking rather than facilitating interaction among welfare mothers, local officials, and other groups of potential supporters or opponents in the city. The two organizers saw this as a regrettable, but necessary, tactic which would: (1) enhance group solidarity and (2) ensure that the welfare mothers would select militant action to fight the system, rather than conventional activities designed to secure public support and approval.

It would not do justice to the complexity of the intermedial process, however, to attribute its emergence in Welfare Mothers Movement groups solely to the actions of the staff members. While some welfare mothers did resent Tina and Leslie's use of the intermedial process to block information and so limit the tactical options available to the women, other recipients welcomed their intermediation in some circumstances. Many active participants in both MWRO and the AFDC League indicated that they did not like having their names known publicly as members of a Welfare Mothers Movement organization largely because they feared harassment from people opposed to welfare. Most welfare mothers also wanted to avoid the conflict and embarrassment that often accompanied interactions across class and sex lines with officials and other members of the elite. For example, one young black MWRO member told me:

> I suppose it gives me an opportunity to see the position that I'm really in. When I talked to the Minnesota state legislator [following an MWRO workshop], that was really bad for me. He asked me questions like I was a child. . . . He was putting me in my place--down!

Contacts initiated by nonrecipients were quickly turned over by many women, therefore, to an organizer or other person available to act as an intermediary. That is an important point to emphasize, for much of the literature on intermediaries assumes that outsiders do something (usually divisive) to the poor (cf. Spicer, 1970). The actions of many welfare mothers in MWRO and the AFDC League, however, suggest that, in at least some cases, the insiders are themselves closely involved in the development of the intermedial process.

As Bailey (1969:175-6) points out, intermediaries
tend to disappear if their monopoly on communication
and control of external or internal resources breaks
down, or if the controlling power decides itself
that it will no longer make use of intermediaries.
It is reasonable to hypothesize that nonrecipient
intermediaries could have disappeared in Minnesota,
therefore. In fact, after MWRO had been functioning
for about a year, a few of the recipient leaders had
developed a number of contacts with influential members of the larger society, particularly welfare
department employees. The women did not use these
relationships for intermedial activity, however, for
the welfare mothers were constrained in this respect
by the same factors which limited Tina's intermedial
activities. They were primarily working class
women who were uncomfortable interacting with people
from the middle class. In addition, recipients were
not neutral and would be expected in conflict situations to support MWRO's goals wholeheartedly. Furthermore, their special knowledge was confined to
the workings of the welfare system and their history
of personal involvement in welfare issues in the
state limited the flexibility and ability to compromise which was central to any use of the intermedial
process to bridge rather than widen the gap between
MWRO and outside organizations. During periods of
conflict, however, Carl Jones and Sam Putnam could
be approached by outsiders because they appeared to
be less directly involved in disputes than the organizers or welfare mothers. These men tended to act
as buffers between the two groups in conflict, while
establishing or maintaining links which could be
used for negotiation or compromise at a later date.

Nor could Bailey's second condition for the disappearance of intermediaries be met, for many of the
city's welfare, political, and economic leaders were
unwilling to forego the use of intermediaries. From
the point of view of outsiders and bureaucrats accustomed to hierarchical and centralized organizations,
MWRO and the other decentralized movement groups
proved perplexing in their own right. Such people
often used intermediaries, then, because they were
not sure of whom else to contact within the group.
For example, at one point a welfare official
stated: "I said I had a dialogue going, but when I
think of the Rights Organization [MWRO], I think of

Sam Putnam. . . . I guess what you are asking is, 'Do
I perceive the Rights Organization as you do?' and I
do not."

In addition, the hostility engendered among welfare
officials by MWRO's attacks on the department was
often aggravated by the same socio-economic and gender differences of which the welfare mothers were
aware. For instance, several welfare administrators
stated during interviews that they felt uncomfortable
around welfare mothers, were disturbed by their lack
of political and organizational experience, or believed the women were incapable of dealing with important issues. This class difference was amplified
by the officials' lack of ease in dealing with the
welfare mothers on a political level, leading one
administrator to burst out in exasperation after a
meeting, "I simply don't know how these women take
me." For these reasons, outsiders often tried to
maneuver middle-class individuals, such as Carl, Sam,
and to a lesser extent Leslie Bernstein, into a position where they might act as an intermediary, even
when they did not wish it.

As can be seen, the simple availability of an intermediary to link two groups together did not guaran-
tee smooth interactions, for there were situations
in which outsiders used an intermediary inappropri-
ately from the point of view of MWRO participants.
For instance, if a nonrecipient tried to deal exclusively with an intermediary when welfare mothers were
present and actively involved in a discussion, such
behavior drew a hostile reaction from the mothers and
a restatement of MWRO's norms that recipients were
the leaders of the group. This evidence supports
Rollwagen's (1974) suggestion that there is an important element of "directionality" in the intermedial
process. Intermediation with the goal of linking
groups together depends for success, in part then,
on being aware of the situations in which the process
must be initiated by the local group or may be begun
by someone from the larger society.

The intermedial activities initiated by the organizers
were used, however, primarily to block contacts between MWRO and outside organizations, to politicize
welfare mothers, and to escalate conflict between
MWRO and other groups. While these actions by the

organizers appeared to be solely divisive to outsiders, they had a positive function as a strategy to maintain a strong ingroup/outgroup orientation. This attitude helped the mothers maintain the high degree of commitment and militancy required by MWRO.

At the same time, an unintended result of the availability of individuals, such as Carl Jones, to take on intermedial activities which <u>linked</u> groups in conflict situations was an increased flexibility in MWRO's political maneuvering. Tina could act as an aggressive leader and attempt to heighten the conflict by disrupting the working of the welfare department because others were ready to step in behind her and work for a compromise when militant action no longer was producing results. Thus Jones' and others intermedial activities served both MWRO's interests by maximizing its chances to win financial grants for its members, as well as the interests of the welfare department by minimizing the chance that conflict would escalate to the point where officials might have to request that their own clients be arrested. As open conflict decreased, more direct linkages between MWRO leaders and welfare officials were formed and the need for intermedial activities by nonrecipients was reduced, although it did not disappear completely. Intermediaries continued to be needed in order to most effectively tap the fluctuating organizational, moral, and legal resources of the larger society; they also served on occasion as links through which opponents and movement groups could covertly cooperate against other groups of opponents (e.g., when the county welfare department surreptitiously aided MWRO in its efforts to delay or defeat the flat grant system being proposed by the state welfare department). Because the ideology of the movement demanded control of the organization by the welfare mothers rather than nonrecipients, both linking and blocking intermedial processes usually took place behind the scenes, especially during conflicts. The use of intermediaries, therefore, tended to be a covert and pragmatic, rather than a normative, process--and one which was not always under the control of the recipients.

This analysis of the sources of opposition and support for the two major Welfare Mothers Movement groups in Minnesota illustrates the difficulties facing a social movement of poor women who have few internal resources such as money, leadership skills, writing or speaking prowess, and no access to conventional political influence (Barkan, 1979:33). Given this lack of internal resources, the welfare mothers had to depend on public support to a greater extent than movements among the "not so poor" or more powerful groups. The need to mobilize often elusive resources from a variety of groups in the larger society, while still formulating meaningful goals for change and maintaining the solidarity and commitment of their members led to a number of organizational and tactical dilemmas, however. The AFDC League and MWRO chose different solutions to these dilemmas, in large part because of the differing institutional and political contexts which faced these two movement groups.

For example, the AFDC League chose goals and tactics which would minimize opposition by prominently engaging in self-help activities and conventional lobbying for limited changes in the state welfare laws. The target institution (elected representatives of the people) was not particularly vulnerable to disruptive tactics or the demands of a special interest group such as welfare mothers. The women were quite concerned with maintaining a favorable public image for welfare recipients, therefore, and with winning the support of groups which could legitimize, publicize, and help them achieve their legislative goals. These goals and tactics were modest in scope and enabled a relatively small number of welfare mothers to obtain limited concessions from welfare and legislative officials and to achieve a measure of success in their efforts toward social mobility.

Ironically, however, the very support which the AFDC League was so successful in gathering may have ultimately contributed to the disintegration of the group. As Gerlach and Hine point out, conflict with the established order facilitates commitment to the movement and continually motivates participants to actively pursue their goals. AFDC League members themselves were aware that the support of outside groups and their own commitment to helping each other return to a mainstream lifestyle had resulted in the most capable women leaving the organization.

MWRO, however, chose a radical strategy which inevitably caused conflict with the earlier Welfare Mothers Movement groups and institutions in the larger society. WRO strategy was based on the assumption that events, such as black riots in the cities, had created a situation in which welfare recipients could coerce officials of the welfare system into granting their demands through the use of militant tactics. MWRO ignored the possible negative reactions of supporters of earlier movement groups, therefore, and sought the backing of more radical groups. In order to pose a real threat to the welfare system through disruption, MWRO also had to focus on building a large organization and membership base, and required a full-time staff to mobilize relatively isolated welfare mothers. Thus MWRO was locked into a cycle of mutual escalation of opposition and commitment among its members.

The large staff and support from militant segments of the larger society created a further problem, however, that of internal conflict over control of the organization. As a result, the staff covertly used the intermedial process to block the flow of information in order to develop a cohesive group solidly opposed to the welfare system and to convince the women that militant (rather than the preferred conventional political) actions were feasible and effective. At the same time, failure to achieve much success through their disruptive tactics led on several occasions to the use of intermediaries who could link MWRO with supporters as well as opponents.

There is, in fact, some contention in the literature over the effectiveness of disruptive activities by the poor and whether there is a need for the poor to seek public support in order to achieve their goals. Piven and Cloward (1977) have argued that efforts to win the support of outside groups tend only to undermine the goals of welfare mothers organizations. They suggest that support from establishment groups or even other social movements diverts the energies of the poor from effective militant tactics to ineffective ones, such as lobbying. Thus, while public support may serve to limit the degree of repression that officials might otherwise employ, they conclude that the poor succeed or fail largely on their willingness to engage in mass defiance and disruption.

Roach and Roach (1978, 1979), however, argue precisely the opposite. From their perspective, welfare mothers pose no threat to the established order through disruption or noncooperation. They suggest that the only hope of improving the status of welfare mothers is through allying themselves with, and working for, the promotion of the lower or working class in general through organized labor.

Neither of these tactics appeared to be totally successful for Welfare Mothers Movement groups in Minnesota; nor does the effect of support or militancy and opposition seem to be related in a simple, direct way with the success or failure of movement organizations. As Gerlach and Hine (1973:190) indicate, "opposition can be utilized, but hardly controlled" and an optimum balance between support and opposition is necessary for the continued spread of a movement. This kind of optimum balance emerged during the late 1960s when groups such as the AFDC League, Direct Action, and early MWRO locals were achieving their somewhat limited successes, but was lost when the financial crises of the 1970s caused fiscal responsibility and restraint to replace the fiscal generosity and political support for the poor which emerged during the War on Poverty.

A number of factors, therefore, played a part in the strategies which were selected by movement groups in Minnesota: (1) the internal attributes of the poor, particularly their lack of resources, such as money or skills, and their fear (whether realistic or not) of reprisals from the established order; (2) the socio-economic and gender differences separating poor women from local elites; (3) the segmented and decentralized nature of movement organizations; (4) changes in the availability of resources and in the amount of opposition to movement groups; and (5) the emergence of specialists, such as intermediaries, to stimulate increased demands by recipients on the welfare system and to provide other important services to welfare mothers as well.

As a result of the interaction between these internal and environmental or contextual factors, Welfare Mothers Movement groups in the state differed in goals, tactics, type of support, and the sources of opposition they experienced. The competition which took place among movement groups may have appeared to weaken the movement at any one point in time, but in the long run proved to be adaptive for the movement as a whole. The variation which existed enabled welfare mothers to tap a wider range of resources and supporters than any one organization could have done, and permitted flexible adaptation to rapidly changing conditions in the larger society. New groups such as the MRA learned from the mistakes of others; failure, in fact, showed what would not, as well as what would, work (Gerlach & Hine, 1973).

FOOTNOTES

1. James Spradley (1974:381) came to the same conclusion about the relationship between "tramps" and the American legal system: "Upon examining the penalties given for public drunkenness, we discover a rather startling fact: the less a man conforms to other American values, the more severe his punishment--not because he violates other laws, but because he does not conform to the values of materialism, moralism and work." This was, of course, the attitude which motivated the members of antiwelfare groups such as WORK.

2. Terms describing the activities of intermediaries have proliferated in the literature. This type of political specialist has been variously labelled a "broker," "gatekeeper," "mediator," and "middleman" (see Snyder, 1976 for a brief review of the ways in which these terms have been used). I will follow Landé's (1977) approach and use "intermediary" as a general term in order both to avoid unnecessarily genderized language and to increase flexibility in observation and analysis. For example, the intermedial activity of any one individual may change temporally or situationally such that someone who acts as a "broker" in one situation may act as a "mediator" in another.

CHAPTER 8

Conclusion

A social movement is a system of interrelated components in which any one aspect cannot be understood
without taking into account all the others; it
is itself a part of an even larger system, the society as a whole. In other words,

> Commitment is closely related to opposition be-
> cause opposition to the movement provides the
> risk situations necessary for bridge-burning.
> It is also related to segmenting organizational
> structure and to the factor of recruitment [for
> commitment increases the ability to recruit
> others, who will in turn go through the commit-
> ment process]. Commitment and ideology are
> intertwined, as commitment is by nature a radi-
> cal shift in values and attitudes. Ideological
> variation is part and parcel of the segmentary
> structure of movement organization, and it in
> turn affects recruitment by offering a wide
> range of types of groups to attract a wide
> variety of potential converts. Opposition to
> a movement is no more monolithic and homogene-
> ous than the movement itself. Hence it is
> linked to organizational segmentation, to dif-
> ferential recruitment potential, and to ideo-
> logical variation. (Gerlach & Hine, 1973:187-8)

Thus the five factors which are crucial for the growth
and spread of a social movement have been isolated
from each other only for the purpose of analysis. In
ongoing human behavior they are interdependent, for
it is the interaction of these factors which produces
the energy that enables movement groups to bring
about personal and social change.

Modification of the Gerlach-Hine Model

The Welfare Mothers Movement was composed of a series
of largely autonomous groups of varying degrees of
formal organization which overlapped to form a local
as well as national movement network--as the Gerlach-

Hine model suggests will be found in all social movements. The most visible of these groups was the National Welfare Rights Organization and its state affiliate, MWRO. The movement as a whole, however, included a number of earlier local groups such as the AFDC League and Direct Action Recipients of Welfare, as well as a later organization, the Minnesota Recipients Alliance. These groups had a wide range of goals and tactics, and occasionally competed with each other for followers, publicity, or financial support.

This variety of groups and the segmentation of the two largest organizations into even smaller neighborhood cells superficially may seem inefficient and a wasteful duplication of effort; the actions of one group occasionally did undermine the efforts of another. When the possibility of error is high-- as it is in human systems such as social movements, however, this variety and even redundancy has a number of positive consequences. The existence of groups ranging from conservative to militant enabled the Welfare Mothers Movement to meet a broad spectrum of psychological and social needs, to draw adherents from a number of different backgrounds, to minimize the failure of one group or strategy, to adapt more effectively to local conditions and problems, and often to escalate the efforts of individuals and groups. In addition, a segmented organization helped movement groups develop political expertise and leadership capabilities among a larger group of welfare mothers than could be accommodated by a single organization.

These decentralized movement groups were characterized by weak leaders who had little ability to compel obedience to unpopular decisions. In general, however, those individuals who were able to control the linkages between the segments within a movement organization and to gather a large body of supporters or faction were in the strongest position to influence the decision-making process. In fact, in larger groups such as MWRO which employed full-time staff members, conflict between the ideal that recipients control the organization and the pragmatic importance of the staff became a major issue. Both leaders and staff members, however, had to make an effort to

develop a consensus of opinion, particularly when
planning external political activities. As a result,
meetings and demonstrations often seemed chaotic to
outsiders and clear decisions were reached with great
difficulty or not at all. The attempt to maximize
the participation of all members in the decision-
making process, however, not only lessened the chance
that welfare mothers would resent or fail to comply
with decisions, but also enhanced morale and the
women's ability to deal effectively with political
issues on their own.

Movement groups were reticulated or linked through
overlapping participation, personal ties between
leaders and staff and through individuals who tra-
velled around the state and nation linking groups
together. Temporary alliances were also formed in
the face of external opposition from the established
order. A shared core of beliefs played a crucial
role in enabling the women to rise above tactical
differences at these times. Thus all participants
agreed that welfare mothers should have the right of
self-determination (to choose between working or
staying home as a full-time mother), the right to be
treated with dignity, and the right to participate
in the political process.

Ideological variation went hand in hand with the segmentation of the movement, however, so that these
core beliefs were expressed in different ways by various movement groups. For example, AFDC League members focused on changing the public stereotype of the
welfare mothers by trying to lead exemplary lives,
by engaging in self-help activities, and by lobbying.
MWRO, on the other hand, formulated a strategy which
attempted to develop group solidarity on the basis
of the women's identity as welfare recipients, as
mothers, and as citizens. Both their identity as
mothers, who had their children's best interests at
heart, and their identity as first-class citizens
implied that political activity was a necessary and
appropriate course of action for the women. Not only
did recipients no longer have to depend on the traditional representatives of the poor (such as social
workers and welfare officials) to represent their
interests in the political process, but MWRO leaders
also believed they could achieve reform through direct
confrontations with the welfare system itself.

The ideology of the Welfare Mothers Movement thus
ran counter to the beliefs in our society which have
confined women to the home and domestic sphere and
which have discouraged not only welfare mothers, but
all women, from taking an important role in politics.
Poor women, however, have additional handicaps which
other women do not face. Welfare mothers as a category were not only physically isolated and scattered
around the city, but also had little to spend on
transportation and the other expenses required for
interaction or political participation with other
recipients. Welfare mothers in Minnesota also were
often socially isolated because there was little
generational dependency in the state and because of
the stigma attached to taking welfare. Many welfare
mothers internalized this negative attitude and
so were often ambivalent about associating with
other recipients (who they feared might actually be
lazy and immoral as the popular stereotype suggested).

For these reasons, recruitment to a Welfare Mothers
Movement group did not occur primarily through significant pre-existing social relationships as the
Gerlach-Hine model hypothesizes. This form of recruitment can only take place where there are heavy
concentrations of potential adherents or nonmove-
ment groups and personal networks already in existence. Due to their social and physical isolation,
however, welfare mothers had to rely primarily on
relatively impersonal methods, such as canvassing
low-income areas and developing favorable media
coverage. These methods not only notified large
numbers of welfare mothers of the existence of movement organizations, but also helped convince them
of the legitimacy and feasibility of their goals.

This kind of support from the media was often very
important for a welfare mother's initial contact
with a movement group, but most continued to fear
reprisals from their worker or harassment by the
general public after joining a movement group.
Nevertheless, interacting with other committed and
highly motivated welfare mothers in small group settings helped many women to overcome their fear and
the effects which desertion or divorce, their inability to support themselves and their children, and
social ostracism had had on their self-image. Welfare mothers who became involved in more militant

groups formed close ties with other participants during demonstrations and experienced the kind of opposition which simply served to quicken and deepen the whole commitment process.

The welfare mothers' perception of the opposition they might face for entering the political arena was an important factor not only in recruitment and commitment to a movement group, but also in the political strategy which was selected. In fact, welfare mothers are more vulnerable than other Americans to reprisals from or control by the elites and other institutions in the established order. Due to their lack of internal resources, the poor are also more dependent on external support to achieve their goals. Early groups such as the AFDC League were especially sensitive to these political disabilities, and attempted to work within the system, thus posing little threat to powerful institutions. They particularly cultivated the support of traditional women's and social work organizations, the welfare department and the general public in order to gain concessions from the legislature and counteract popular stereotypes.

After the disruptions of the mid-1960s, however, more militant tactics and far-reaching demands were perceived as a feasible and effective strategy against an increasingly vulnerable welfare system. The federal government and other national and local radical elites seemed willing to tolerate or even encourage such activities, and groups such as Direct Action and MWRO emerged to take advantage of the new organizational, legal, and moral resources which were being made available to the poor. The conflict which these organizations advocated, however, led to a number of dilemmas. The use of disruptive tactics caused a temporary split with the conservative segment of the movement and was instrumental in the development of the intermedial process--which had appeared in only rudimentary form in earlier groups. This process was used behind the scenes both to link welfare mothers to supporters and opponents across class and sex boundaries, and covertly to block the flow of information and communication between the movement and external organizations in order to escalate intergroup conflict.

177

The optimum balance between opposition and support which had resulted in the proliferation of Welfare Mothers Movement groups, however, was lost during the "benign neglect" of the Nixon years and the New Federalism of the mid-1970s (i.e., those federal policies such as revenue sharing which were designed to ease urban fiscal crises by enlarging the role of state and local officials in setting policy and funding priorities). The Welfare Mothers Movement and other segments of the urban poor responded to these changes in the external context by a retrenchment to the local level. In Minnesota, this change was reflected in the emergence of the MRA and a renewed focus on and sensitivity to local, rather than national, problems and politics (Fiske, 1979:164-5).

Thus, with the exception of the primary mode of recruitment, the analysis of the Welfare Mothers Movement in Minnesota has provided substantial support for the validity of the five factors which were identified by the Gerlach-Hine model as crucial for the spread of a movement. This combination of factors effects a rapprochement between the focus of traditional social movement research on internal features, such as participants' values and ideology, and the new emphasis in the resource mobilization literature on external support and constraints. In addition, Gerlach and Hine contribute to the development of the resource mobilization perspective as well by identifying the positive role which opposition to a movement may play. Thus by raising the commitment level of participants, an optimum level of opposition tends to generate leadership capacity, "turns ex-leaders into martyrs, provides grist for the ideological mill, enhances the commitment and recruitment potential of other participants, generates new leadership from the small interaction groups, and is a force against which to unite the movement's disparate segments" (Gerlach & Hine, 1973:184-5).

By characterizing the total movement as a network, the Gerlach-Hine model enables the observer to go beyond a single organization to an analysis of the movement as a whole. It also frees us from some of our cultural biases about the expected or most "efficient" form of organization, the "proper" role of ideology, and the "inevitable" effect of factionalism or consensual decision-making. In particular,

the use of an anthropological approach, such as Gerlach and Hine's, is one way in which social scientists
can move beyond a priori assumptions that the behavior
and organizations of minorities, the poor, lower
classes, or other races are inadequate and pathological. This perspective and its commitment to cultural
relativism requires both a coming to terms with the
social organization (rather than social disorganization or failure) of groups outside the mainstream of
our society (Guillemin, 1975:298), and an awareness
of the ongoing interaction of these groups with segments of the larger society.

The Movement Was More than Welfare Rights

This has been a case study of the Welfare Mothers
Movement, focusing on Minneapolis and the state of
Minnesota, and thus has included some of their
unique characteristics as explanatory variables.
This case material is a valuable addition to the literature on the movement, therefore, for most of the
previous analyses have been restricted to a single
organization within the movement, NWRO, and to the
form and politics of that organization in large
urban areas of the northeastern United States.

On the basis of this fairly narrow geographical and
organizational range of movement groups, Piven and
Cloward (1977) have emphasized racial and class variables as key factors which explain the movement.
For example, they state:

> Blacks became indignant over their condition--
> not only as an oppressed racial minority in a
> white society, but as poor people in an affluent
> one. The civil rights victories being won in
> the South would, after all, be of greatest ben-
> efit to southern blacks who were already in,
> or were prepared to enter the middle class. . .
> but poor urban blacks had little to show for
> it. (Piven & Cloward, 1977:269)

The approach to the Welfare Mothers Movement which
has been taken here does not in any way attempt to
refute Piven and Cloward's (1971) early work in which
they convincingly outline the role of the federal
government, the Civil Rights Movement, and the racial

disturbances of the 1960s in stimulating the emergence of many organized groups of welfare mothers. Nor does it dispute the importance of class and racism as general explanatory variables for understanding the activities of welfare mothers in other parts of the country. Indeed, class differences and the disabilities associated with poverty have been given a central place in this analysis. Race, however, has had but little relevance to the Welfare Mothers Movement in Minnesota.

Most observers have suggested that NWRO was largely a black welfare mothers organization. In 1972, Martin (quoted in Piven & Cloward, 1977:317) estimated that 85 percent of NWRO's members were black, 10 percent were white, and 5 percent were Latin. In Minnesota, on the other hand, the welfare rolls were 82 percent white, 8 percent black and 7 percent Indian (the remaining 3 percent being recorded "other" or unknown) (Minnesota Department of Public Welfare, 1969). My estimate of the racial composition of MWRO suggests that approximately 70 percent were white and 30 percent were black; racial percentages closely approximated those of the state welfare rolls, however, when earlier groups such as Direct Action Recipients of Welfare and the AFDC League (including the Indian AFDC League) were included in the estimate. Thus this racial balance, the lack of a history of racial problems and the absence of large ghettos in the urban areas of the state explain some of the differences found between the movement in the Midwest and the East Coast.

Piven and Cloward also give a prominent place in their analysis to the effects of lower class status on the activities of organized welfare mothers. Yet Roach and Roach, in their critical review of Piven and Cloward's theory, provide an example of a class-based analysis carried to an extreme. They argue that Marxist theory indicates--and their own analysis of social movements among blacks, women, welfare clients, and other deprived groups confirms--that welfare mothers groups on their own can achieve only limited gains. They advocate an alliance with the working class:

> Categories such as "blacks" and "women" obscure
> class differences between members of the partic-

ular category. . . . Pretending greater unity
than actually exists has weakened these movements. . . . What we have proposed is that
activists concentrate their efforts on strength-
ening the power of the organized working class
vis-a-vis capital. (Roach & Roach, 1979:268-9)

Roach and Roach suggest that all the categories of
the poor would benefit from winning working class
demands for more jobs, a shorter work week, and free
day care or health services. Unfortunately, the
experience of NWRO showed that the working poor were
not interested in allying with the dependent poor,
nor were they drawn into the organization through
the multi-issue programs developed by NWRO (e.g., by
organizing campaigns on day care issues, health care,
housing, etc.) (Piven & Cloward, 1977:316). Nor has
it been the experience of blacks or women that general advances in the labor market are translated
into advances for them. As Blau (1979:277-82) points
out, there are two distinct labor markets--one male
and one female--and the latter is economically de-
pressed in terms of unemployment and women's share in
the total earned income in proportion to their pro-
ductive contribution. Women, whether black or white,
continue to predominate in those jobs that are least
secure, least subject to unionization, least lucra-
tive, and least conducive to career advancement (Stone,
1979:579). Thus Roach and Roach's conclusion that
the Welfare Mothers Movement should be treated exclusively as a problem of class conflict seems unwarranted.

This is not to deny, however, that problems of poverty and racism can partially explain the growth of
Welfare Mothers Movement groups, the goals and tactics which were selected, and the successes and failures they experienced. The exclusive interest of
Piven and Cloward as well as others in these two variables, however, has obscured the impact of a third
variable which was more apparent in Minnesota where
the factor of racism was relatively unimportant.

Feminism: The Gender Variable

This third variable was the impact of sexism on the
politics of the Welfare Mothers Movement. The failure of analysts to examine the effect of traditional

sex roles and stereotypes on the movement stems in part from the fact that acknowledging gender differences has been seen by the participants and intellectuals of both the New Left and the black movement as potentially divisive. For example, Freeman (1979: 562) has reported the unremitting hostility expressed by most of the men and some early feminists of the New Left at the prospect of an independent women's movement which was not tied to radical ideology. In the same vein, Stone (1979:585-6) argues:

> The view that racism is the sole cause of black female subordination in America today exhibits a very simplistic view of the black female condition. . . . Because color, gender, and wealth are at present collective determinants of power and privilege in America, it is almost impossible to disentangle their individual effects. Thus, those who would assert that the elimination of one type of social discrimination should have priority over all others display a naive conceptualization of the nature of power in American society and the multi-faceted character of social oppression.

What is unique about the Welfare Mothers Movement, then, is the way in which race, poverty, and gender variables have interfaced to develop a double and occasionally triple handicap on the political activities of poor women.

In spite of the welfare mother's general lack of overt awareness of the impact of sexism, gender differences did play an important role in the dynamics of the movement. The women unconsciously responded to and manipulated sexist attitudes in a number of ways. The manner in which gender intersected with class (and elsewhere with race) was particularly apparent in: (1) the ideology of the movement; (2) the formation of, or rather the failure to form, alliances; and (3) the recruitment process.

The welfare mothers' commitment to traditional sex roles, which is associated with their predominantly working-class origins, was most apparent in the earliest group, the AFDC League. These women were not only committed to these sex roles, but their tactics and goals were designed to exemplify this commitment. The group, therefore, was limited in the kind of social or personal change which it could advocate. A dilemma faced the welfare mothers of later groups, such as MWRO, however. They continued to identify with traditional roles embodied in the terms, "mothers" and "ladies," yet these seemed to conflict with the group's insistence upon achieving political power based on their identity as "citizens." The strong verbal support movement participants gave to these conventional sex roles, however, helped resolve their ambivalence about the time they devoted to movement activities, provided the women with a highly salient identity as a basis for group solidarity, and attached a certain respectability to their activities (which would have been denied on the basis of the negative stereotype of the welfare mother).

Movement ideology was linked to the welfare mothers' failure to establish potentially useful alliances with local feminist organizations as well. Contact on the national level was also minimal, being limited, for example, to having Gloria Steinem address the NWRO convention in 1971. The Welfare Mothers Movement, however, being ideologically committed to establishing the respectability of its members, was unlikely to be attracted to another movement which at that time often denigrated traditional female roles and was publicly engaged in a gay/straight factional struggle in which lesbianism was presented as the essential feminist idea (Freeman, 1979:558; 567). Furthermore, both branches of the feminist movement were composed of predominantly white, middle-class, and college-educated women; thus, there was an obvious class difference between the two movements. Welfare mothers were not just ordinary members of the working or lower classes either--they were a special despised subgroup avoided by other women simply because they were public dependents. This kind of class barrier was only aggravated by the racial differences which could be found between feminist and some welfare mothers organizations.

Finally, class, gender, and racial factors affected the recruitment process characteristic of movement groups in Minnesota. Traditional sex roles have isolated women in their homes, and such isolation

can be amplified, not only by poverty but also by
the disgrace of welfare. Racial differences are an
additional source of discontinuity in the network of
relations among many groups of poor women. As a result, largely impersonal means of recruitment had to
be utilized, rather than significant, pre-existing
relationships. It is possible, however, that within
some large black or ethnic communities, pre-existing
networks might serve as links through which welfare
mothers could be recruited to a movement group in the
manner suggested by the Gerlach-Hine model.

This analysis of the Welfare Mothers Movement offers
insight into three major variables which had an impact on the politics of a special category of poor
women in our society. As such, this study not only
corrects some of the inaccuracies and omissions in
previous analyses of this movement, but also adds
to our understanding of the changes which took
place as a result of the growth of the Welfare
Mothers Movement.

A Decade of Change?

It is often difficult to assess a movement's effect
on society until after it has ceased to exist. Many
movements arise within an established order, flour-
ish for a while, and then disappear--but they seldom leave the established order unchanged (Gerlach
& Hine, 1973).

The activities of Welfare Mothers Movement groups
in the decade between 1965 and 1975 did bring about
significant change in American society. For example,
the traditional relationship between welfare officials and recipients was altered as the women began
to reject the passive and subordinate roles previously assigned to them. This new assertiveness
often produced tangible benefits as well, by acting
as a check on the actions of caseworkers and by
enabling welfare mothers to learn about and so manipulate the system to their own advantage.

Movement activity also led to change in a number of
welfare laws. For example, the illegality of the
man-in-the-house rule and the right to have a third
party accompany a welfare mother at appeals or

termination hearings were established through litigation stimulated by the movement. Legal change was not restricted to redress through the courts, however, but also involved attempts to influence legislation. Thus, the AFDC League successfully lobbied to allow children past the age of 18 to remain on the grant if they were still attending school; MWRO and the Minnesota 87 alliance helped to defeat the proposed 10 percent reduction in welfare funding in 1971. On the national level, NWRO lobbied against FAP. While efforts of movement participants may or may not have significantly affected the outcome of these issues, the women _were_ exercising their rights as citizens to become involved in the political process--a fact which was not lost on legislators, administrators, and members of the general public.

Finally, the publicity which was sought by most movement groups, and which inevitably accompanied their more militant activities, certainly had an impact on the broad area of public opinion. Undoubtedly some of this impact was negative, for the goals of movement groups were not always clearly or accurately reported by the press, nor would they have received a sympathetic hearing among certain segments of the population in any case. Nevertheless, as many outsiders pointed out, the activities of movement groups, such as the AFDC League, did provide an alternative to the traditional negative stereotypes which had prevailed before. While generating more initial opposition, even MWRO's militant actions and demands eventually convinced some people of the validity of the new identities and "rights" of welfare mothers.

The success of movements must be judged not only in terms of their stated goals of bringing about social change, however, but also in terms of their ability to bring about personal transformation in the lives of their participants (Gerlach & Hine, 1973:180). Although these personal or private goals and successes were at variance with the group-oriented ideology of organizations, such as MWRO, it is fruitless to argue that one is more important than the other or that personal change should precede social change or vice versa. Many welfare mothers were able to achieve real though small gains through their participation in movement groups. These benefits ranged from experiencing a feeling of heightened self-esteem or becoming more comfortable with their choice to remain at home as full-time mothers, to special financial grants, getting an education or job training, or developing contacts with other welfare mothers as well as influentials in the local political arena.

The lessons of the feminist movement in particular should caution us not to dismiss such change as inconsequential. Indeed, as Freeman (1979:561) points out, "From a sociological perspective, the [superficially nonpolitical rap group was] probably the most valuable contribution of the women's liberation movement to the tools for social change." Such groups (which were structurally equivalent to the locals and satellite groups of the Welfare Mothers Movement) served: (1) to bring previously isolated women together in a situation where they could interact with one another, compare experiences, and develop common concerns; and (2) to generate personal change directly through the process of "consciousness-raising." This process altered the woman's perception of both herself and society at large, while developing the sense of solidarity which was crucial to the spread of the movement as well.

Thus the Welfare Mothers Movement did bring about a measure of political and personal change among many poor women who were effectively excluded from traditional women's or working class organizations, and who were not directly touched by the appeal of the feminist movement itself. The disappearance of the Welfare Mothers Movement in the mid-1970s, however, does not mean that the movement failed completely. For both individual participants as well as institutions in the established order (while not overthrown or replaced) were different than they would have been had the Welfare Mothers Movement never existed.

BIBLIOGRAPHY

Aberle, David. "A Note on Relative Deprivation Theory
as Applied to Millenarian and Other Cult Movements" in Reader in Comparative Religion, William
A. Lessa and Evon Z. Vogt, eds. New York:
Harper and Row, 1965.

Adams, Karen L. and Ware, N.C. "Sexism and the English
Language" in Women: A Feminist Perspective, 2nd
ed. Jo Freeman, ed. Palo Alto, CA: Mayfield
Publishing Co., 1979.

AFDC League. A Manual for AFDC Recipients (mimeographed), 1966.

American Broadcasting Company. The Anatomy of Welfare.
April 14, 1971. (Television Broadcast)

Bailey, F.G. Strategems and Spoils: A Social Anthropology of Politics. Oxford: Basil Blackwell, 1969.

Barkan, Steven E. "Strategic, Tactical, and Organizational Dilemmas of the Protest Movement against
Nuclear Power," in Social Problems 27(1):19-37.

Beck, Bernard. "Bedbugs, Stench, Dampness and Immoral-
ity: A Review Essay on Recent Literature About
Poverty," in Crisis in American Institutions, J.
Skolnick and E. Currie, eds. Boston: Little,
Brown & Co., 1970.

Bernard, Jessie. "The Mother Role" in Women: A Feminist Perspective, Jo Freeman, ed. Palo Alto,
CA: Mayfield Publishing Co., 1979.

Blau, Francine E. "Women in the Labor Force: An
Overview" in Women: A Feminist Perspective, Jo
Freeman, ed. Palo Alto, CA: Mayfield Publishing
Co., 1979.

Cloward, Richard A. and Elman, Richard M. "Poverty,
Injustice, and the Welfare State," in Crisis in
American Institutions, J. Skolnick and E. Currie,
eds. Boston: Little, Brown & Co., 1970.

Collier, Jane F. "Women in Politics," in Women in
Culture and Society, M.Z. Rosaldo and L. Lamphere,
eds. Stanford, CA: Stanford University Press, 1974.

Eames, Edwin and Goode, J.G. (eds.). Urban Poverty:
A Crosscultural Context. New York: Free Press, 1973.

Eames, Edwin and Goode, J.G. Anthropology of the City. Englewood Cliffs, NJ: Prentice-Hall, Inc., 1977.

Elman, Richard M. The Poorhouse State. New York: Random House, 1966.

Fiske, Shirley. "Urban Indian Institutions," in Urban Anthropology 8(2): 144-71, 1979.

Freeman, Jo. "The Women's Liberation Movement" in Women: A Feminist Perspective, Jo Freeman, ed. Palo Alto, CA: Mayfield Publishing Co., 1979.

Friedrich, Paul. "Introduction to Part III: The Political Middleman," in Local-level Politics, Marc J. Swartz, ed. Chicago: Aldine Publishing Co., 1968.

Gamson, William A. The Strategy of Protest. Homewood, IL: Dorsey Press, 1975.

Garretson, Lucy. "The ERA: Law, Custom, and Change," in Anthropology and the Public Interest, Peggy R. Sanday, ed. New York: Academic Press, 1976a.

-----. American Culture: An Anthropological Perspective. Dubuque, IA: Wm. C. Brown Co., 1976b.

Gelb, Joyce and Sardell, Alice. Strategies for the Powerless: The Welfare Rights Movement in New York City. Unpublished paper prepared for delivery at the American Political Science Association meetings in New Orleans (mimeographed), 1973.

Gerlach, Luther and Hine, Virginia. People, Power, Change: Movements of Social Transformation. New York: The Bobbs-Merrill Co., Inc., 1970.

-----. Lifeway Leap: The Dynamics of Change in America. Minneapolis, MN: University of Minnesota Press, 1973.

Ginsberg, Mitchell I. "The State of Society," in Social Work in Practice. Fourth NASW Symposium, Oct. 1975, Bernard Ross and S.K. Khinduka, eds. Washington, DC: National Association of Social Workers, Inc., 1976.

Gouldner, Alvin. "The Secrets of Organizations," in Readings in Community Organization Practice, R. Kramer and H. Specht, eds. Englewood Cliffs, N.J.: Prentice-Hall, Inc., 1969.

Guillemin, Jeanne. Urban Renegades: The Cultural Strategy of American Indians. New York: Columbia University Press, 1975.

Gurr, T.R. Why Men Rebel. Princeton, NJ: Princeton University Press, 1970.

Hacker, Helen M. "Women as a Minority Group," in Women: A Feminist Perspective, 2nd ed., Jo Freeman, ed. Palo Alto, CA: Mayfield Publishing Co., 1979.

Handler, Joel F. Reforming the Poor: Welfare Policy, Federalism, and Morality. New York: Basic Books, Inc., Publishers, 1972.

Hertz, Susan H. "The Politics of the Welfare Mothers Movement: A Case Study," in Signs: Journal of Women in Culture and Society 2(3):600-11, 1977.

-----. "The Institutional Context and Political Organizations Among Welfare Recipients in Minneapolis," in South Atlantic Urban Studies, vol. 2: 123-40, 1978.

-----. Disruption and Adaptation: A Social Movement Among Welfare Mothers, Unpublished manuscript, 1980. (Available from Anthropology Department, 2112 G St., N.W., The George Washington University, Washington, D.C., 20052).

Hoffer, Eric. Minneapolis Tribune, Oct. 24, 1968.

Hoshiro, George. "Conceptual Analysis of the Nixon Welfare Proposal," in Social Casework 51(3): 157-66, 1970.

Jacobs, Paul. "Keeping the Poor Poor," in Crisis in American Institutions, J. Skolnick and E. Currie, eds. Boston: Little, Brown & Co., 1970.

Jenkins, J. Craig. "What Is to Be Done: Movement or Organization?" in Contemporary Sociology 8(2): 222-8, 1979.

Johnson, Betty S. and Holton, Carol. "Social Work and the Women's Movement," in Social Work in Practice, Bernard Ross and S.K. Khinduka, eds. Washington, D.C.: National Association of Social Workers, Inc., 1975.

Jones, Delmos J. "Incipient Organizations and Organizational Failures in an Urban Ghetto," in Urban Anthropology 1(1):51-67, 1972.

Kaplan, Harvey L. "Organization of AFDC Mothers," in _Minnesota Welfare_ 5(2-3), 1966. (Mimeographed publication of the Minnesota Department of Public Welfare, St. Paul, MN)

Klein, Philip. _From Philanthropy to Social Welfare: An American Cultural Perspective_. San Francisco: Jossey-Bass, Inc., 1968.

Kurzman, Paul (ed.). _The Mississippi Experience: Strategies for Welfare Rights Action_. New York: Association Press, 1971.

Landé, Carl H. "Introduction: The Dyadic Basis of Clientelism," in _Friends, Followers, and Factions_, S.W. Schmidt, L. Guasti, C.H. Landé, and J.C. Scott, eds. Berkeley: University of California Press, 1977.

Leacock, Eleanor. "Introduction," in _The Culture of Poverty: A Critique_, E. Leacock, ed. New York: Simon and Schuster, 1971.

Liebow, Elliot. _Tally's Corner: A Study of Negro Streetcorner Men_. Boston: Little, Brown & Co., 1967.

Lewis, Oscar. "The Culture of Poverty," in _Scientific American_ 215(4):19-25, 1966.

Martin, George T. _Organizing the Underclass: Findings on Welfare Rights_. Working paper no. 17. Human Side of Poverty Project, Department of Sociology, State University of New York at Stony Brook, 1971.

-----. _The Emergence and Development of a Social Movement Organization Among the Underclass: A Case Study of the National Welfare Rights Organization_. Unpublished Ph.D. dissertation, Department of Sociology, University of Chicago, 1972.

Martin, M. Kay and Voorhies, Barbara. _Female of the Species_. New York: Columbia University Press, 1975.

McCarthy, John D. and Zald, Mayer N. "Resource Mobilization and Social Movements: A Partial Theory," in _American Journal of Sociology_ 82(6):1212-41, 1977.

McCourt, Kathleen. _Working-Class Women and Grass-Roots Politics._ Bloomington, IN: Indiana Univ. Press, 1977.

190

McFee, Malcolm. Modern Blackfeet: Montanans on a Reservation. New York: Holt, Rinehart & Winston, 1972.

Minnesota Department of Public Welfare, SMSA, 1969.

Minter, Steven A. The Executive's Role in Today's Climate of Dissent. Paper presented at the Minnesota Welfare Association Conference, March 18, 1970.

Moynihan, Daniel P. The Negro Family: The Case for National Action. Washington, DC: U.S. Department of Labor, 1965.

Nicholas, Ralph W. "Factions: A Comparative Analysis," in Political Systems and the Distribution of Power, Michael Banton, ed. New York: Barnes & Noble, Inc., 1968.

-----. "Social and Political Movements," in Annual Review of Anthropology, B.J. Siegel, A.R. Beals, and S.A. Tyler, eds. Palo Alto, CA: Annual Reviews, Inc., 1973.

Parker, Seymour. "Poverty: An Altering View," in To See Ourselves: Anthropology and Modern Social Issues, Thomas Weaver, ed. Glenview, IL: Scott, Foresman & Co., 1973.

Piven, Frances F. and Cloward, Richard A. Regulating the Poor: The Functions of Public Welfare. New York: Pantheon Books, 1971.

-----. Poor People's Movements: Why They Succeed, How They Fail. New York: Random House, 1977.

Roach, Jack L. and Roach, Janet K. "Disunity and Unity of the Working Class: Reply to Piven and Cloward," in Social Problems 26(3):267-70, 1979.

Rollwagen, Jack. "Mediation and Rural-urban Migration in Mexico: A Proposal and a Case Study," in Latin American Urban Research 4:47-63, 1974.

Rosaldo, Michelle. "Woman, Culture and Society: A Theoretical Overview," in Woman, Culture and Society, Michelle Rosaldo and Louise Lamphere, eds. Stanford, CA: Stanford Univ. Press, 1974.

Rothman, Gene H. Welfare Rights Groups of the 1930s and 1960s. Unpublished master's thesis, Department of Sociology, Columbia University, 1969.

Sacks, Karen. "Engels Revisited: Women, the Organization of Production, and Private Property," in *Woman, Culture, and Society*, Michelle Rosaldo and Louise Lamphere, eds. Stanford, CA: Stanford University Press, 1974.

Sanday, Peggy R. "Female Status in the Public Domain," in *Woman, Culture and Society*, M. Rosaldo and L. Lamphere, eds. Stanford, CA: Stanford University Press, 1974.

Schneider, David and Smith, Raymond T. *Class Differences and Sex Roles in American Kinship and Family Structure*. Englewood Cliffs, NJ: Prentice-Hall, Inc., 1973.

Smelser, Neil. *Theory of Collective Behavior*. New York: Free Press, 1963.

Snyder, Peter Z. "Neighborhood Gatekeepers in the Process of Adaptation: Cross-ethnic Commonalities," in *Urban Anthropology* 5(1): 35-52, 1976.

Spicer, Edward. "Patrons of the Poor," in *Human Organization* 29: 12-20, 1970.

Spradley, James P. "Beating the Drunk Charge," in *Conformity and Conflict*, 2nd edit., James P. Spradley and David W. McCurdy, eds. Boston: Little, Brown & Co., 1974.

Stack, Carol. *All Our Kin: Strategies for Survival in a Black Community*. New York: Harper & Row, Publishers, Inc., 1974.

State of Minnesota. *Public Welfare Manual*. St. Paul: The Department of Public Welfare, 1957.

-----. *Statistical Summary of Public Assistance*. St. Paul: Department of Public Welfare, Jan. 1965.

Steiner, Gilbert Y. *The State of Welfare*. Washington, DC: The Brookings Institution, 1971.

Stone, Pauline T. "Feminist Consciousness and Black Women," in *Women: A Feminist Perspective*, 2nd edit., Jo Freeman, ed. Palo Alto, CA: Mayfield Publishing Co., 1979.

Swartz, Marc J., Turner, Victor W., and Tuden, Arthur, eds. *Political Anthropology*. Chicago: Aldine Publishing Co., 1966.

Ten Broek, Jacobus. "The Two Nations: Differential Moral Values in Welfare Law and Administration," in Crisis in American Institutions, J. Skolnick and E. Currie, eds. Boston: Little, Brown & Co., 1970.

Tilly, C., Tilly, L. and Tilly, R. The Rebellious Century: 1830-1930. Cambridge, MA: Harvard University Press, 1975.

Valentine, Charles A. The Culture of Poverty: Critique and Counterproposals. Chicago: University of Chicago Press, 1968.

Wallace, Anthony F.C. "Revitalization Movements," in American Anthropologist LVIII: 264-81, 1956.

Walz, Thomas H. Toward the Year 2000: Restructuring and Retooling Social Work for the 1970s. Paper given at the Minnesota Welfare Conference, March 16, 1970.

Waxman, Chaim I., ed. Poverty: Power and Politics. New York: Grosset & Dunlap, 1968.

Wheeldon, P.D. "The Operation of Voluntary Associations and Personal Networks in the Political Processes of an Inter-ethnic Community," in Social Networks in Urban Situations, J.C. Mitchell, ed. New York: Humanities Press, 1969.

Whitaker, William. The Determinants of Social Movement Success: A Study of the National Welfare Rights Organization. Unpublished Ph.D. dissertation, Florence Heller School for Advanced Studies in Social Welfare, Brandeis University, 1970.

Wolf, Eric R. "Kinship, Friendship, and Patron-Client Relations in Complex Societies," in A.S.A. Monograph #4, The Social Anthropology of Complex Societies, M. Banton, ed. New York: Barnes & Noble, Inc., 1968.

DATE DUE